THE WAY OF THE RABBIS:

An Introduction To Rabbinics For Young People

by
Rabbi Aaron H. Blumenthal
and
Ann Helfgott

edited by
David R. Blumenthal

UNITED SYNAGOGUE OF AMERICA
COMMISSION ON JEWISH EDUCATION

Published by the
United Synagogue of America
Commission on Jewish Education
155 Fifth Avenue, New York, New York 10010
ISBN: 0-8381-3126-3

for my mother

The heart of her husband trusted in her
and he lacked no good thing.
(Proverbs 31:11)

TABLE OF CONTENTS

Introduction 6

Chapter One: Holiness 9

Chapter Two: The Family 15

Chapter Three: The Poor and the First Fruits 24

Chapter Four: The Study of Torah 36

Chapter Five: Social Violence 47

Chapter Six: The Power of Words 55

Chapter Seven: The Old and the Stranger 62

INTRODUCTION

My father believed strongly that education was the core of life. To be ignorant was an act of stupidity. There was no excuse for a person not to learn. And so he spent most of his life studying and teaching—in the classroom, in the pulpit, and in his writing. Learning and instruction was his *raison d'être*.

But—and it was an important "but"—learning was not a matter of rote; education was not an attempt to accumulate an endless quantity of facts. True learning was challenging the text, questioning what one was taught. One scrutinized respectfully but one *never* avoided an honest question. "Do you really believe that God wants to reinstate sacrifices? If not, why pray for that?" "Do you really believe that the misogyny of the rabbis is worth preserving?" "Did anyone ever really practice an eye for an eye?" And so on. It was not only "What does the text actually say?" but "How did the tradition deal with it?" *and* "How ought *we* to deal with it?". Text and its interpretation was life.

Rabbinics was always my father's first love. He loved Talmud and it pained him that no really good method has ever been developed to teach rabbinics to young people who were not brought up in the yeshiva world. Beginning rabbinics is probably the most difficult subject in our curricula. He experimented with various methods and welcomed anyone's innovations. He was particularly impressed with the methods developed by Professor Jacob Neusner for studying and teaching rabbinic texts.

In an attempt to combine his love for rabbinics and the teaching thereof with his provocative approach to education in general, my father published (at age 67) his first book, *If I Am Not For Myself* (United Synagogue of America, Commission on Jewish Education, 1973), which is a study of the personality and work of the great talmudic sage, Hillel. In it, he sets forth all the legends and concerns, and then he urges the reader to question and to probe them, always bearing in mind the great moral teachings that the tradition attributes to Hillel. After retirement, he went to work on other books. One, lamentably, was left too fragmentary to retrieve. The other is this book, *The Way of the Rabbis: An Introduction to Rabbinics for Young People*. In this book, my father again tries to solve the problem of how to teach the great rabbinic tradition to students who will not be studying Gemara five to twenty hours a week. (For a broader statement of my father's method in study and in the rabbinate, cf. ". . .

and bring them closer to Torah": The Life and Work of Rabbi Aaron H. Blumenthal, ed. D. Blumenthal, Ktav, 1986.)

The method of this book is quite simple. It begins with the assumption that the student has already read Chapter 19 of the Book of Leviticus, the so-called Holiness Code. Reading the thirty-seven verses of that chapter, however, does not exhaust its wisdom. This book, then, does two things: (1) It cites rabbinic texts on those verses. With this, the book intends to: (a) introduce students to original rabbinic texts, (b) show how the rabbis of the Talmud approached the biblical text, and (c) raise certain ethical and moral questions relating to both the biblical and the rabbinic quotations. (2) After introducing the rabbinic texts, the book urges the readers to raise their own textual and ethical questions and to discuss these thoroughly.

The book is divided into seven chapters: Holiness, The Family, The Poor and the First Fruits, The Study of Torah, Social Violence, The Power of Words, and The Old and the Stranger. The chapters, thus, follow the sequence of the biblical text. My father did this purposely. As he wrote: "This method of study is somewhat like the one in which we imagine the Rabbis of the Talmud themselves engaged. One particular verse of Torah leads to a discussion of other related verses and the various commentaries available upon all these verses. This, in turn, leads to a discussion of the implications to individuals and to the Jewish people as a whole."

A word about the structure of this book: Each chapter is composed of a group of texts given in Hebrew and of comments given in English and Hebrew. The method of presentation is simple: Each text has a reference and a footnote number. The footnotes refer to the comments in the English section of the chapter. The references point to the source from which the text is taken. In this way, the student has exposure to an original-language text, a discussion of the text, and a reference for further study.

My father insisted that the texts be given in the original Hebrew, without translation, so that students should learn that minimal amount of rabbinic Hebrew and style which they contain. In his commentary, he points out and explains some of the rabbinic idioms, explicates difficult concepts, and poses questions for discussion. The comments are largely intended for the instructor or group leader. It helps if the leader is learned but it is not necessary. A little preparation is all that is needed. It is even conceivable that students themselves could take this text and use it on their own.

Finally, my father intended that this book be used for a whole semester or for a short youth-group weekend. It can be part of a regular curriculum or used as a taste of rabbinics for a short study session.

My father's favorite source was the *Encyclopedia Talmudit*. His second favorite source was the *Torah Sheleymah* by Kasher. The reader who wishes to locate further material or fuller references should consult these extraordinary reference books.

My father will perhaps be best known for his long fight within the Conservative movement on behalf of women's rights. He wrote the original *teshuva* permitting *aliyot* for women in 1954 and authored numerous articles on this issue (see *". . . and bring them closer to Torah,"* 11-24, 25-42, 145-62). However, he lived and wrote in a time before the widespread use of egalitarian language. Hence, in this book, he uses "man" and not "humanity" or "humankind," and always uses the impersonal masculine pronouns. I have respected this stylistic device though my father certainly meant to include women in every use of "man" (cf. e.g., the beginning of Chapter Two).

A word of deep thanks is due to Ms. Ann Helfgott, my cousin, who wrote the last chapter. Ann received an M.A. in Jewish Education from the Jewish Theological Seminary of America and spent several years in Israel on various programs. She is now married and a mother, a member of the Board of the Solomon Schechter School of Suffolk County, and a Hebrew calligrapher by profession. I remember that, for her wedding, she asked for (and received) a Talmud! Ann has done a very good job in writing Chapter Seven and in designing the cover. I thank her.

My father's life-long companion was my mother. She shared his triumphs, and she encouraged him and gave him strength when his spirits flagged. She supported him in his rabbinate and patiently typed endless drafts of his books, even doing some of the research for them. It is fitting, therefore, that this book be dedicated to her.

Learn the tradition and question it. Use the mind on the tradition. This was my father's way. If the student can learn this method for *Vayikra* 19, he or she can use it for any biblical pericope. This was my father's hope: that this method would be applied to the study of the *parashat ha-shavu'a* and that further textbooks like this would be written. If this book succeeds as a modest beginning, his efforts will have been well rewarded.

David R. Blumenthal
Atlanta, GA
Rosh ha-Shana 5748

CHAPTER ONE: TEXTS
פרק ראשון: קדושה

א. **דבר אל עדת בני ישראל** (ויקרא י״ט, ב׳). מלמד שהפרשה הזאת נאמרה בהקהל. ומפני מה נאמרה בהקהל, מפני שרוב גופי תורה תלוין בה (ויקרא רבה כ״ד, ה).[1]

ב. **קדושים תהיו** (שם). הוו פרושים מן העריות ומן העבירה. שכל מקום שאתה מוצא גדר ערוה אתה מוצא קדושה (שם כ״ד, ו).[2]

ג. **קדושים תהיו** (שם). אם אתם מקדשים עצמכם, מעלה אני עליכם כאילו קדשתם אותי (שם).[3]

ד. **אחרי ה׳ אלהיכם תלכו** (דברים י״ג, ה). מאי דכתיב **אחרי ה׳ אלהיכם תלכו**. וכי אפשר לו לאדם להלך אחר שכינה . . . אלא להלך אחרי מידותיו של הקב״ה. מה הוא מלביש ערומים, דכתיב **ויעש ה׳ אלהים לאדם כתנות עור וילבישם** (בראשית ג, כ״א), אף אתה הלבש ערומים.[4]

הקב״ה ביקר חולים, דכתיב, **וירא אליו ה׳ באלוני ממרא** (בראשית י״ח, א), אף אתה בקר חולים.

הקב״ה ניחם אבלים, דכתיב, **ויהי אחרי מות אברהם ויברך אלהים את יצחק בנו** (בראשית כ״ה, י״א), אף אתה נחם אבלים.

הקב״ה קבר מתים, דכתיב, **ויקבר אותו בגי** (דברים ל״ד, ו), אף אתה קבר מתים (סוטה י״ד, א).

ה. **את כל עדת** (שמות ל״ה, א-ב) . . . **ששת ימים** (שמות ל״ה, א-ב) למה נאמר. לפי שנאמר **ועשו לי מקדש** (שמות כ״ה, ח), שומע אני בין בחול בין בשבת . . . ת״ל (תלמוד לומר) **ויאמר אלהם . . . ששת ימים תעשה למלאכה**, בחול ולא בשבת (מכילתא דר׳ ישמעאל, פרשת ויקהל).[5]

ו. **ויקהל משה** (שמות ל״ה, א). אמר להם הקדוש ברוך הוא לישראל. אם אתם נקהלים בכל שבת ושבת לבתי כנסיות ולבתי מדרשות, וקוראין בתורה ובנביאים, מעלה אני עליכם כאילו המלכתם אותי בעולמי שכן נאמר, **אתם עדי נאם ה׳, ואני אל** (ישעיהו מ״ד, ח). אתם מעידים עלי שאני אלוה בעולם (תנחומא, תורה שלמה, שמות ל״ב, סימן ה׳).[6]

CHAPTER ONE: HOLINESS

(1) דבר אל כל עדת בני ישראל

This is the first Rabbinic comment encountered by the class and it illustrates a basic element in the Rabbis' approach to the Torah. They read the text very carefully and if they detected anything out of the ordinary, they paused to try to understand it.

A good way to approach many Rabbinic comments is to ask, "What bothers the Rabbis about this verse?" In this particular case, students should go back to the first chapter of *Vayikra* and to chapters 11 through 18, and read the first verses. God speaks to Moses, to Aaron and his sons, to the Children of Israel, but this time the words אל כל עדת are used. They are superfluous. The sentence loses none of its meaning without them. This is what bothered the Rabbis. Why did God use the words אל כל עדת?

This question is based upon another of their fundamental beliefs . . . the Divine Revelation of the Torah. Since God wrote the Five Books of Moses, any deviation from the norm is not accidental but deliberate and He wanted the Rabbis to search and speculate about the meaning of anything unusual in the text.

The Rabbis concluded that the extra words אל כל עדת meant exactly what they say . . . that everybody was gathered together to hear the proclamation of this chapter. This was done only once before in *Shemot* 25:1-3, which the class should read. Why are these words used here?

(a) Because most of the essential *mitzvot* of the Torah are summarized in it. As the student keeps studying this chapter, he will notice that this is so.

(b) Because the essence of Judaism is the striving for holiness and the first sentence in this chapter voices this call to holiness.

The purpose of this course is to convey the beliefs and teaching of the Rabbis. Students are free to voice their own opinions and to challenge those held by the Sages. But, basically, there is little disagreement about the ideas held by the Rabbis about the origin of the Torah.

The word "holy" is not a popular term in America today. However, if we want to understand either Biblical or Rabbinic Judaism, we must open our minds to their ideas. The Torah calls upon us several times to be holy, and most often it offers a reason . . . because God is holy.

Read *Vayikra* 11:45 in class. God took Israel out of Egypt to be our God and He requires us to be holy because He is holy. Also read *Vayikra* 20:7 and 20:28.

Members of the class may be more familiar with *Bemidbar* 15:40. The number of repetitions of the call to be holy is significant. Add to them the Rabbinic comments and we find ourselves engaged in a very important *mitzvah*.

The class might discuss the meaning of holiness. Does it apply to individual people? to objects? Is the Torah Scroll holy? Rabbi Judah Hanasi was called רבי יהודה הקדוש. What does this mean?

Are members of the class familiar with holiness in other religions? Holy relics in Christianity, pieces of the cross, of the shroud, etc.? In India one sees "holy men" in all kinds of positions and garb.

What is holiness in Judaism? The subject of holiness is a very difficult one. We shall not be able to do more than discuss it superficially:

(a) One of the names of God is הקדוש ברוך הוא. Holiness is an attribute of God.

(b) Man is called upon to do two things: to be holy himself, and to declare the holiness of God. A mourner who recites the קדיש every day sanctifies the name of God with the words, יתגדל ויתקדש. Whenever a Jew prays alone at any service and on any day of the year, he recites the words . . . אתה קדוש ושמך קדוש. The class should read this *berakhah* in the *Siddur* (*Sim Shalom*, p. 110). Whenever a Jew prays with a *minyan* and the Cantor repeats the *Amidah*, the Congregation rises to recite the *kedushah* (*Sim Shalom*, p. 170) which contains the words קדוש קדוש קדוש.

In these and other ways, man declares the holiness of God in prayer every day of the year. But how does man make himself holy?

The world which the Rabbis knew was steeped in paganism and immorality. There was no sense of sin about immorality. It was an accepted way of life. Therefore, the Rabbis identified holiness with separating oneself from the values and practices of the pagan world. Man's striving for holiness in Judaism involves the rejection of immorality, wickedness and evil.

God is holy and the Jew proclaims His holiness to the world every day. Man is born with the potential for holiness. He must strive for it and the first step is to reject all evil.

---

(3) מעלה אני עליכם

This paragraph is the other side of the coin . . . the performance of good deeds. One can almost hear the reasoning of the Rabbis . . . God is holy and He wants us to be holy, but how does He express His holiness? If we could answer that question, we might do the same thing as we search for holiness in our lives. How does God act out His holiness?

The class should be encouraged to read and report on the mythologies of Egypt, Rome, Greece etc. They will learn that all the ancient gods lied, cheated and betrayed each other. Judaism taught not only that God was One, but that He was the essence of goodness, compassion, mercy etc., i.e., holy. And He required man to be holy like Him.

---

(4) מה הוא . . . אף אתה

One other thing is to be noted. For God and for man, holiness consists, in part, of involving oneself in the needs of others. Or, to turn it around, one cannot achieve holiness by abandoning others or by removing oneself from the world. Other religions have monasteries where one can retreat from the world in order to concentrate upon acquiring a state of holiness through reflection, prayer, fasting, meditation or other self-discipline. In Judaism, there is no such isolation.

The Bible references are:

(a) *Bereshit* 3:32.

(b) *Bereshit* 18:1. The previous chapter ends with the circumcision of Abraham, and the Rabbis say God came to visit him during his recuperation.

(c) *Bereshit* 25:11.

(d) *Devarim* 34:4-6.

---

(5) ששת ימים

This is the only other time in the Torah that the words כל עדת are used. It is not God who speaks here but Moses, and the phrase is used twice. It occurs at the beginning of Chapter 35 in *Shemot* and the class should read verses 1-5. The next few sentences are too difficult, but they should be read in English.

The most important event in the wanderings of our ancestors in the desert, next to the acceptance of the Ten Commandments at Sinai, was the building and utilization of the Tabernacle. Strange things happened within the Tabernacle and later in both Temples. The priests were expected to violate the Sabbath! Special animal sacrifices were offered and the priests had to slaughter and sever the various parts and burn them on the altar, acts which were forbidden elsewhere.

The question then arose as to whether, in the building of the original Tabernacle or the Temples, it had been permissible to work on the Sabbath. The Rabbis concluded that the act of building the Temple did not supersede the laws of the Sabbath.

---

(6) אתם עדי

This is the second time that we encounter the phrase מעלה אני עליכם. When man sanctifies himself, God considers it as if he had added to the holiness of God. And when we assemble to study holy books, it is as if we have crowned Him King of His universe.

This runs counter to all our ideas about God. God is holy; He is King of the universe. Can anything that we do add to His Holiness or to His Kingship? The question seems ridiculous, for it implies that at this very moment you and I can add to God's sovereignty and holiness. Impossible!

Yet that is precisely what the Rabbis assert. God's holiness is incomplete and man (perhaps, only man) can make it complete.

This is a very difficult concept and should not be pushed. We will

13

encounter it again. The teacher might ask what this does to our concept of man.

This idea finds further expression on the High Holy Days, when our prayers proclaim that God is King only when men proclaim Him so.

CHAPTER TWO: TEXTS
פרק שני: המשפחה

איש אמו ואביו תיראו (ויקרא י״ט, ג).

א. **איש:** אין לי אלא איש.[1] אשה מניין? כשהוא אומר **תיראו,** הרי כאן שנים. א״כ (אם כן) מה ת״ל (תלמוד לומר) **איש?** איש סיפק בידו לעשות, אשה אין סיפק בידה לעשות מפני שרשות אחרים עליה. נתאלמנה או נתגרשה, שניהם שווים (קדושין ל, ב).

ב. אין לי אלא אבות, אמהות מניין? ת״ל **ואת** (שמות כ, י״ג) ואין אתין אלא אמהות, שנאמר **שמה קברו את אברהם ואת שרה אשתו** (בראשית מ״ט, ל״א) (מקור לא ידוע, אבל ראה ספרי פר׳ של״ג, שנ״ג).[2]

ג. **את** אביך (שמות כ, י״ב) — זו אשת אביך (מכילתא דרשב״י, תורה שלמה שמות כ, סימן רצ״ז-רצ״ט).
    ואת אמך (שם) — זו בעל אמך (שם).
    ואת — לרבות אחיך הגדול (שם).
    ואת — לרבות אחיך הבכור (שם).[3]

ד. בני בנים הרי הם כבנים (שם).[4]

ה. נאמר: **כבד את אביך ואת אמך,** ונאמר: **כבד את ה׳ מהונך** (משלי ג, ט). השווה הכתוב כבוד אב ואם לכבוד המקום (מכילתא, תורה שלמה, שמות כ, סימן רצ״ד).[5]

ו. נאמר: **איש אמו ואביו תיראו** (ויקרא י״ט, ג). ונאמר: **את ה׳ אלוהיך תירא ואותו תעבוד** (דברים ו, י״ג; י, כ). השווה מורא אב ואם למורא המקום (קדושין ל, ב).

ז. שלשה שותפין הם באדם, הקב״ה (הקדוש ברוך הוא), אביו ואמו. בזמן שאדם מכבד את אביו ואת אמו אמר הקב״ה מעלה אני עליהם כאילו דרתי ביניהם, וכבדוני (שם).

ח. בזמן שאדם מצער את אביו ואת אמו אמר הקב״ה יפה עשיתי שלא דרתי ביניהם. שאלמלא דרתי ביניהם ציערוני (שם ל״א, א).[6]

ט. רבי אומר: גלוי וידוע לפני מי שאמר והיה העולם, שבן מכבד את אמו יותר מאביו, מפני שמשדלתו בדברים. לפיכך הקדים הקב״ה כיבוד אב לכיבוד אם. וגלוי וידוע לפני מי שאמר והיה העולם, שהבן מתיירא מאביו יותר מאמו, מפני שמלמדו תורה. לפיכך הקדים הקב״ה מורא האם למורא האב (שם).[7]

י. גדול הוא כיבוד אב ואם שהעדיפו הקב"ה יותר מכבודו. נאמר **כבד את אביך ואת
אמך**, ונאמר **כבד את ה' מהונך**. ממה אתה מכבדו? ממה שחננך. מפריש לקט
שכחה פאה . . . ועושה סוכה ולולב ושופר ותפילין וציצית ומאכיל את העניים ואת
הרעבים . . . אם יש לך, אתה חייב בכולן ואם אין לך אין אתה חייב באחת מהן. אבל
כשהוא בא אצל כיבוד אב ואם, בין שיש לך הון, ובין שאין לך הוֹן כבד את אביך
ואת אמך, אפילו שאתה מסבב על הפתחים (פסיקתא רבתי כ"ג, כ"ד).[8]

י"א. איזהו מורא? לא ישב במקומו, ולא ידבר במקומו, ולא יסתיר דבריו. איזהו כבוד?
מאכיל ומשקה, מלביש ומנעיל, מכניס ומוציא (קדושין ל"ב, א).

י"ב. מכבדו בחייו ומכבדו במותו. מכבדו במותו כיצד? היה אומר דבר שמועה מפיו, לא
יאמר כך אמר אבא, אלא כך אמר אבא מורי . . . והני מילי תוך שנים עשר חדש.
מכאן ואילך אומר זכרונו לברכה (קדושין ל"א, ב).[9]

י"ג. עד היכן כבוד אב ואם? אמר להם (עולא) צאו וראו מה עשה עובד כוכבים אחד
באשקלון, ודמה בן נתינה שמו. פעם אחת בקשו חכמים פרקמטיא בששים ריבוא
שכר, והיה מפתח מונח תחת מראשותיו של אביו ולא ציערו (שם ל"א, א).[10]

י"ד. פעם אחת היה יושב לבוש סירקין של זהב. והיה יושב בין גדולי רומי, באתה אמו
וקרעתו ממנו, וטפחה על ראשו, וירקה לו בפניו, ולא הכלימה (שם ל"א, א).

ט"ו. **ואת שבתותי תשמרו** (ויקרא י"ט, ג). יכול יהא כיבוד אב ואם דוחה שבת. ת"ל **איש
אמו ואביו תיראו ואת שבתותי תשמרו אני ה'**. כולכם חייבים בכבודי (יבמות ה,
ב).[11]

ט"ז. מניין שאם אמר לו אביו היטמא, או שאמר לו אל תחזיר אבידה לא ישמע לו? ת"ל
איש אמו ואביו תיראו ואת שבתותי תשמרו, כולכם חייבים בכבודי (ב"מ ל"ב, א).

י"ז. האב חייב בבנו למולו, ולפדותו, וללמדו תורה, ולהשיאו אשה, וללמדו אומנות.
רבי אליעזר אומר אף להשיטו במים. רבי יהודה אומר כל שאינו מלמד את בנו
אומנות, מלמדו לסטות. ליסטות סלקא דעתך? אלא כאילו מלמדו ליסטות (קדושין
כ"ט, א).[12]

CHAPTER TWO: THE FAMILY

(1)   אין לי אלא

The phrase . . . אין לי אלא followed immediately by מניין . . . is a standard formula among the Rabbis. Its purpose is to raise questions and it occurs often. To understand it, however, we have to distinguish three steps in the process.

(a) *What the Torah says:* Here the text reads איש. That means that the *mitzvah* to revere one's parents devolves upon איש and איש alone.

(b) *The question which the Rabbis raise:* Here, it is אשה מניין. They are attempting to extend the observance of the *mitzvah* to women as well.

(c) *The proof:* The use of the plural תיראו in the verb is sufficient. Note that the proof comes from the same verse in the Torah.

The teacher might approach this text with "what bothers the Rabbis about this verse?" Obviously it is the singular noun (איש) and the plural verb (תיראו).

All these three steps must be present in the formula: (a) the Bible text, (b) the Rabbinic query and (c) the proof. We can demonstrate this with another example. The class should turn to *Vayikra* 26:42 which is to be read in the original. The repetition of the word את intrigued the Rabbis and they made the comment in item (ב) of the student's text.

---

(2)   אבות . . . אמהות

The Rabbis here broaden the concept of *Avot*. The three steps required are obvious. (a) Torah text: את . . . את . . . את . . .; (b) the Rabbinic query: מניין אמהות; and (c) the proof: אין אתין אלא אמהות.

Thus, God's covenant with the Patriarchs is extended to include the Matriarchs as well! On Rosh Hashanah and Yom Kippur, we pray זכור לנו ברית אבות. We also invoke the זכות אבות. In both cases we call to mind the goodness and virtues of the Matriarchs, as well as those of the Patriarchs.

This extension of the Covenant is achieved by the Rabbis through a lesson derived from the little word את. Again one notes that the proof is found in a Torah verse.

Such recourse to the word את to expand the law is another formula employed frequently by the Rabbis. Turn to *Shemot* 20:12. In the Ten Commandments we read כבד את אביך ואת אמך. What can the words את and ואת mean here?

Let's begin with some questions. What should be the attitude of children towards their father's wife who is not their mother? Do they owe her any respect? Biblical society was polygamous. Should children show deference to their father's other wives? Or, if either parent dies and the surviving parent remarries, how should the child (of any age) behave towards the step-parent? Modern society has witnessed an explosion in the number of divorces. If one's parents have divorced and one or both remarry other partners, how should the child act towards these new partners?

There should be much lively class discussion on these questions. The reading of the Rabbinic text should be deferred until after the class discussion.

We have had two examples of Rabbinic expansion of the law of the Torah by interpreting the almost insignificant word את. Does this seem reasonable? Or is it stretching the text too far?

Here we encounter one of the unique emphases in Judaism. The core component is the text, the Torah; nothing else comes close to it in importance—not even God! God is the Author of the Torah, and having revealed it to man, the Rabbis imagine God saying: אלו אותי עזבו ותורתי שמרו.

Though Judaism speaks of loving God and having faith in Him, the fundamental objective of Jewish living is to observe the laws of the Torah. The Torah becomes the great source which the Rabbis interpreted in order to expand the law. For something new to be legitimate, it had to be derived from the Torah.

Judaism does not say "have faith" or "believe" or "follow My prophet." It says "obey the Torah."

Now, the Torah is not a big book. Its Five Books contain only 5845 verses. Much of it is history, folklore and poetry. This leaves a very narrow foundation upon which to erect a whole legal, moral and ethical system. The question of stretching the text should be considered within this imperative to find authority in the Torah.

Two great sages, Rabbi Akiba and Rabbi Ishmael, differed about that. Rabbi Ishmael believed that דברה תורה כלשון בני אדם. When two humans speak to each other, good grammar requires the use of the word את before a direct object. The Torah also used good grammar. Therefore, את should not be used for any other purpose. Rabbi Akiba argued that the Torah, as the speech of God, contained many clues to additional learning and it was legitimate and even necessary to derive logical extensions of the law from the word את, every time it occurred in the Torah. He did the same thing with the word גם.

Students might be asked to write reports on Rabbi Ishmael and Rabbi Akiba.

---

(4) בני בנים

This is a good opportunity to discuss the closeness of Jewish family life which has been responsible for higher standards of morality, lower crime rates, etc., among Jews in all countries including the USA. Which traditional values and observances tend to bring the family together? Are there "Jewish" virtues still characteristic of contemporary Jews? Are modern Jews close to their families?

---

(5) השווה הכתוב

Some of the ideas about God taught by the Rabbis are highly unusual. Most of us think of God as majestic, exalted and so superior to man that there is no comparison between the greatness of God and the insignificance of man.

This is one of the basic themes of the High Holy Days, the contrast betwen God's greatness and man's utter frailty. The class might read the ונתנה תוקף to illustrate this contrast.

But that is not everything the Rabbis said. In their careful scrutiny of the text, they noticed that God employed the same verb roots (ירא, כבד) to command the honoring and reverence of Himself and the honoring and reverence of parents. This, of course, was deliberate and it bothered the Rabbis. Why did God do that? And they conclude that He meant to equate the honoring of parents with the honoring of Himself. Does this diminish the greatness of God? Does it elevate the stature of man? What does this tell us about the Rabbinic concept of man?

---

(6)   כבדוני . . . ציערוני

This carries the Rabbinic concept of God and man almost beyond the conceivable. Again the teacher must ask what this *midrash* does to our understanding of God.

Obviously the Rabbis are exalting parenthood, but it is all part of their glorification of man. (See (ז) in the student's text—God is not only the Creator of the species, man, but the partner of parents in fashioning every human being.)

This elevation of the *mitzvah* to honor parents beyond that of honoring God is unique to Judaism. One cannot imagine a clergyman of any other faith putting God and man in this relationship to each other.

---

(7)   אביו . . . אמו

This statement of the Rabbis draws a distinction in the relationship of children between their mothers and fathers. Social conditions have changed since then. What difference do modern children see in the roles played by their respective parents? The teacher might assign as a project: "How my parents felt about their mothers and fathers."

---

(8)   מורא . . . כבוד

This statement draws a clear distinction between the financial and the personal obligations of children. Some of the unhappiest people are those whose children are paying for their care in nursing homes for the aged, but who never or rarely are visited by their children or grandchildren.

A discussion about how to honor one's deceased parent should prove to be interesting. Students probably will be familiar with the ritual observances: *kaddish*, *yahrzeit*, tombstone, and the giving of charity, etc. In some communities there probably are substantial memorials in hospitals, synagogues, lectureships, even chairs of Judaica to commemorate the dead. Students might be sent on a search for such memorials in their communities. Less well known is the *mitzvah* to study on a *yahrzeit*. It is interesting that among Jews the memory of great men is perpetuated by observing their *yahrzeits*, not their birthdays. The *yahrzeit* of Moshe Rabbenu is listed on many calendars (Adar 7th).

A *yahrzeit* is not a sad day. It is an opportunity to perform a number of *mitzvot* such as the giving of charity, prayer and study, and to recall the good deeds of the deceased. Among Hassidim, the *yahrzeit* of a "Rebbe" is a happy celebration.

In some communities, the *yahrzeit* of a deeply-beloved person who had served the community faithfully is observed regularly. Is there anyone whose *yahrzeit* the class, as a whole, should observe?

Some of the laws of *avelut* may be taught here at the teacher's discretion.

The spirit of the child's conduct is more important than the act itself. The Talmud tells of a son who fed his father pheasants every day but spoke so boorishly that he failed to observe the *mitzvah* of כבוד אב. On the other hand, another son who worked at a grindstone set his father at this difficult task, but thereby did fulfill the *mitzvah*. Government agents came to take the father away for forced labor which was more strenuous. The son, who was not at this work, was able to substitute for the father.

R. Abbahu boasted that his son, Abimi, really fulfilled the precept of honoring parents. Though Abimi had five sons in his father's lifetime, when R. Abbahu came and called out at the door, Abimi himself speedily went to open it for him, crying "Yes, yes," until he reached it.

R. Tarfon, who was a very rich man and had many servants, had a mother. When she wished to get into bed, he would bend down and let her stand on his

21

back to ascend. When she wished to descend, she also stepped down on him first. His mother went down to walk in the courtyard of the house one Sabbath and her shoes tore and slipped off. He placed his hands beneath her soles and she walked on them until she reached her bed.

When R. Joseph heard his mother's footsteps, he would say "I arise before the approaching *Shekhinah*."

One of the most beautiful stories which I have witnessed is that of a son whose aged father resided in a local nursing home. The son visited the father almost daily and on Shabbat morning they sat together in the synagogue. The father was not always alert and did not always remember the prayers. The son would bend down to his father's ear during the Amidah in the hope that the father, too, might be able to daven.

Students might be assigned a project to draw up suggestions about the spirit and the letter of the relationship of children to parents and grandparents. Their parents also may be invited to submit their suggested rules. The lists should be exchanged and discussed anonymously.

At some point in this chapter, the class should draw up a list of modern problems in child-parent and family relationships. The question really is how far the teachers should carry the project. Some problems are never discussed except within peer groups, which is sad. The bride who says, "This is *my* wedding" and proceeds to ignore every other member of her family in the arrangements; the couple that decides to elope; the student who drops out to "find himself," etc. should be discussed in class long before the problems arise.

---

(11) כולכם חייבים בכבודי

How absolute is the commandment to obey one's parents? The Rabbis make it very clear that there are limits. The parent is not to be obeyed if he demands that the child violate God's law. What bothers the Rabbis here? The fact that the law about the Sabbath follows immediately after honoring parents. But what if the parent demands that the child just do something foolish?

This is only an introduction to the responsibilities of parents to children. Providing food, clothing and shelter are not even mentioned. The class might discuss how far parents should go in sacrificing for their children, or how much children may permit their parents to sacrifice for them. Are parents obligated to pay for children's college education? Should children work to help, even if the parents can well afford it?

פרק שלישי: הנדכאים והביכורים

לא תכלה פאת שדך לקצור (ויקרא י"ט, ט).

א. אלו דברים שאין להם שעור הפאה, והבכורים, והראיון, וגמילות חסדים ותלמוד
תורה. אלו דברים שאדם אוכל פרותיהם בעולם הזה, והקרן קיימת לו לעולם הבא:
כבוד אב ואם, וגמילות חסדים, והבאת שלום בין אדם לחברו, ותלמוד תורה כנגד
כולם (פאה א, א).[1]

ב. אין פוחתים לפאה מששים. ואף על פי שאמרו אין לפאה שעור, הכל לפי גודל
השדה, ולפי רוב העניים, ולפי רוב העניה (פאה א, ב).[2]

ג. נותנים פאה מתחילת השדה ומאמצעה (פאה א, ג).[3]

ד. שלש אבעיות ביום: בשחר, ובחצות, ובמנחה (שם ד, ה).[4]

ה. הזורע את שדהו מין אחד, אף על פי שהוא עושהו שתי גרנות, נותן פאה אחת.
זרעה שני מינין אף על פי שעשאן גורן אחת, נותן שתי פאות. הזורע את שדהו שני
מיני חטין, עשאן גורן אחת, נותן פאה אחת. עשאן שתי גרנות, נותן שתי פאות (שם
ב, ה).[5]

ו. מעשה שזרע רבי שמעון איש המצפה לפני רבן גמליאל, ועלו ללשכת הגזית ושאלו.
אמר נחום הלבלר: מקובל אני מרבי מיאשה שקבל מן הזוגות, שקבלו מן הנביאים,
הלכה למשה מסיני, בזורע שדהו שני מיני חטין, אם עשאן גורן אחת פאה אחת.
שתי גרנות, נותן שתי פאות (שם ב, ו).[6]

ז. בעה"ב (בעל הבית) שהיה עובר ממקום למקום, וצריך ליטול לקט שכחה ופאה
ומעשר עני, יטול. וכשיחזור לביתו ישלם. דברי ר"א (רבי אליעזר). וחכ"א (וחכמים
אומרים) עני היה באותו שעה (שם ה, ד).[7]

ח. מי שיש לו מאתים זוז יטול לקט שכחה ופאה ומעשר עני (פאה ח, ח).[8]

לעני ולגר תעזוב אותם (ויקרא י"ט, י).

ט. הפאה אין בה טובת הנאה לבעלים. מאי טעמה? עזיבה כתיב בה (חולין קל"א, ב).[9]

ובקצרכם את קציר ארצכם (ויקרא י"ט, ט).

י. אמר רבי אבדימוס ברבי יוסף. מה ראה הכתוב לתנם באמצע הרגלים, פסח ועצרת
מכאן, וראש השנה ויום הכפורים וחג מכאן? ללמדך שכל הנותן לקט, שכחה ופאה
ומעשר עני כראוי, מעלה עליו הכתוב כאילו בית המקדש קיים ומקריב קרבנות
לתוכו. וכל שאינו נותן כראוי מעלה עליו הכתוב כאילו בית המקדש קיים ולא
הקריב קרבנות לתוכו (תו"כ).[10]

י"א. **קציר ארצכם** ולא קציר חוץ לארץ (ירושלמי פאה פ"ב ה"ה).

בכורים.[11]

י"ב. אין מביאין ביכורים חוץ משבעת המינין (בכורים א, ג).

י"ג. אלו מביאין ולא קורין: הגר מביא ואינו קורא, שאינו יכול לומר **אשר נשבע ה'
לאבותינו לתת לנו** (דברים ו, כ"ג) ואם היתה אמו מישראל מביא וקורא. וכשהוא
מתפלל בינו לבין עצמו אומר "אלוהי אבות ישראל." וכשהוא בבית הכנסת אומר:
"אלוהי אבותיכם". ואם היתה אמו מישראל אומר: "אלוהי אבותינו" (שם א, ד).

י"ד. תני בשם רבי יהודה: גר עצמו מביא וקורא. מה טעם? כי **אב המון גוים נתתיך**
(בראשית י"ז, ה)[12] לשעבר היית אב לארם, ועכשיו, מכאן ואילך, אתה אב לכל
הגוים. רבי יהושע בן לוי אמר הלכה כרבי יהודה (ירושלמי בכורים פ"א, ה"ד).

ט"ו. גר מביא וקורא שנאמר לאברהם, **אב המון גוים נתתיך.** הרי הוא אב כל העולם
כולו. לאברהם היתה השבועה תחילה שירשו בניו את הארץ (מבוסס על משנה
בכורים א, ד ובריתא בכורים ה"ד).

ט"ז. כיצד מפרישין הביכורים. יורד אדם בתוך שדהו ורואה תאנה שבכרה, אשכול
שבכר, ורמון שבכר, קושרו בגמי ואומר: "הרי אלו בכורים" (בכורים ג, א).

י"ז. כיצד מעלין את הבכורים . . . (שם ג, ב).[13]

י"ח. בראשונה כל מי שיודע לקרות, קורא. וכל מי שאינו יודע לקרות, מקרין אותו.
נמנעו מלהביא התקינו שיהיו מקרין את מי שיודע ואת מי שאינו יודע (שם ג, ז).[14]

י"ט. **שלש פעמים בשנה יראה כל זכורך את פני האדון ה'** (שמות ל"ד, כ"ג). הכל חייבים
בראיה חוץ . . . וקטן, ונשים, ועבדים, . . . והחולה, והזקן, ומי שאינו יכול לעלות
ברגליו. איזהו קטן? כל שאינו יכול לרכוב על כתפיו של אביו ולעלות מירושלים אל
הר הבית, דברי בית שמאי. ובית הלל אומר, כל שאינו יכול לאחוז בידו של אביו
ולעלות מירושלים להר הבית . . . (חגיגה ב, א).[15]

כל זכורך

כ. להוציא את הנשים. שאינן חייבות. אבל הן עולות עם בעליהן מפני שמחת יום טוב.
(לקח טוב, תורה שלימה, שמות ל"ד, סי' קסג).[16]

כ"א. לרבות את הקטן. מכאן אמרו כל קטן שיכול לאחוז בידו של אביו ולעלות
מירושלים להר הבית חייב להעלותו (מדרש הגדול, תורה שלימה, שם, סי' קס"ד).

אל פני האדון ה' (שמות כ"ג, י"ז).

כ"ב. עבדים פטורים מן הראיון. דכתיב: **יראה כל זכורך אל פני האדון ה'**, מי שאין לו
אלא אדון אחד, יצא זה שיש לו אדון אחר (חגיגה ד, א).

כ"ג. מי שחציו עבד וחציו בן חורין עובד את רבו יום אחד ואת עצמו יום אחד, דברי בית

25

הלל. אמרו להם בית שמאי, תיקנתם את רבו ואת עצמו לא תיקנתם. לישא שפחה אינו יכול, בת חורין אינו יכול. ליבטל? והלא לא נברא העולם לא לפריה ורביה. שנאמר **לא תהו בראה לשבת יצרה** (ישעיהו מ״ה, י״ח). אלא מפני תיקון העולם כופין את רבו ועושה אותו בן חורין, וכותב לו שטר על חצי דמיו. חזרו בית הלל הורו כבית שמאי (חגיגה ב, א).[17]

CHAPTER THREE:
THE POOR AND THE FIRST FRUITS

We will not be commenting on every verse in *Vayikra* 19. The teacher has the option of teaching verses 4-8 or skipping them. Our next comment is on verses 19: 9-10.

---

(1)   לקט שכחה פאה

All three basic readings should be taught at the beginning of the lesson, with special emphasis upon the terms לקט, שכחה, פאה. This Biblical text is among the most important building blocks for Jewish communal responsibility for the poor, the stranger, the widow and the orphan. They should be discussed fully. They are a matter of law and *mitzvah* in Judaism, not merely the voluntarism of charity.

Rabbinic logic is unique. Its basic classic, the Mishnah, was not committed to writing until the year 200 C.E. at the earliest. Prior to then, everything was transmitted orally. Therefore, the material is arranged so as to facilitate memorization.

Item (א) illustrates the point well. It is the first statement in the Mishnah which teaches the laws of *peah*. It wants to say that there is no limit to the amount of *peah* one may or ought to give. And it does say so, but then, for the purposes of easier memorization, it collects other matters which have no limit and lists them all together. Rabbinic style calls for a generalization here. "These are the things which . . ." "אלו דברים".

Having mentioned גמילות חסדים and תלמוד תורה in the list, the author seems to have recalled another list in which they are included. This leads to another identical generalization. "These are the things in which . . ." "אלו דברים".

Elaborate as our society is, it has not been able to solve the problem of poverty. Programs which succeed in one year may fail in another. That is why the Mishnah contradicts itself about how much one should give, and then bases it upon the economic circumstances at any time and place.

This is an excellent opportunity to discuss the whole problem of poverty. Members of the class may want to comment upon the American welfare system. It would be wise to have the class draw up a list of benefits provided by the welfare system for the old, the young, the incapacitated, the handicapped, the unemployed, etc. One should emphasize that these are legal rights enacted by Congress to discharge society's obligations to the unfortunate.

It should be indicated that practically none of this existed before the Great Depression of 1929. Students also may want to read about Poor Laws in England in the *Encyclopedia Britannica* for purposes of comparison.

Over the centuries, Jews have developed a reputation for taking care of their own. When the first Jews came to New Amsterdam in 1764, Peter Stuyvesant demanded that they assume full responsibility for their poor and sick, which they did gladly.

But how did poverty begin altogether? *Bereshit* 48: 13-27 describes the process in Egypt, though it is much older. The class can, and should read it in the original, noting each step in the process of enslaving the Egyptian people.

This story explains how the feudal system was established in Egypt. It omits, however, the money-lender and the slave trader, both of whom flourished in all ancient societies.

An impoverished farmer would borrow money. Interest rates were so high that he fell deeper and deeper in debt. He then was forced to sell his wife and childen into slavery, then his land and ultimately himself. Society then split into two classes, the rich landowners and the poor serfs.

The Torah proclaims four laws which interrupted this vicious cycle which led to the enslavement of the poor.

(a) It outlawed the payment of interest: *Shemot* 22:24, *Vayikra* 25: 35-37, *Devarim* 23:20.

(b) It ordained the *Shmittah* Year, *Devarim* 15: 1-2, 7-11, which cancelled all debts.

(c) It instituted the Jubiliee Year, *Vayikra* 25: 1-13, which returned the land to the family of the original owners.

(d) It placed limits upon the years of service of Hebrew slaves: *Shemot* 21: 1-2, *Devarim* 15: 12-15.

The class should familiarize itself with these laws and discuss them fully. Each of them has a special contribution to make to the establishment of a wholesome society whose people feel themselves to be equal and free.

It would take us very far afield if we were to add Rabbinic comment to these laws. However, there are two things to be noted:

(a) The Biblical laws and some of the Rabbinic additions reflect an agricultural society. The poor are sustained from the produce of the soil and, when property is returned to the members of the original family, it is agricultural land that is involved. Cancelling a debt which a farmer owes his neighbor does not impose a great hardship on the creditor.

Vayikra 25: 23-30 summarizes the Jubilee Year and then raises the problem of property within a walled city. This should be read and noted. It is the beginning of a transition to urban living.

(b) In the Rabbinic period, there was a more complex society. When a farmer borrows or lends money, it is either for food or for seed. In the city, people borrow money to do business. Men deposit money in banks which lend the money to make money.

Now the problem was whether a system to help the poor in an agricultural community could be adapted to function in an urban society, freeing men to develop their economy and to care for the indigent under the new circumstance. That they succeeded is an indication of the genius of the Rabbinic process.

---

(3) נותנים פאה

The technical term for this support of the poor is *pe'ah* which means "corner". However this should not deter a generous farmer from leaving more of the produce of his field. He is not limited to what grows in the corners.

---

(4) שלש אבעיות

The dignity of the poor is to be maintained. The farmer cannot be expected to stand at the gate of his field to permit the poor to enter whenever they choose to appear there. But neither should they be forced to wait until such time as it pleases him to admit them. A fixed time is set, which makes it mutually convenient.

---

(5) הזורע את שדהו

This is another expansion of the law of *pe'ah*. The farmer is to give his due for every type of grain in his fields even if they do not reach to the corners. In reaping the field, he naturally separates the two kinds of produce and sets aside *pe'ah* for each.

The problem arises when he has planted two varieties of the same grain. The solution depends upon his treatment of the two varieties. If he co-mingles them, it is obvious that there is no distinction between them. However, if he separates them, they are to be treated as diverse grains and require *pe'ah* from each.

---

(6) מעשה שזרע ר' שמעון

This is a story told to reenforce the ruling in the previous paragraph. A law stated anonymously is strengthened considerably if an actual case is cited which sustains it. That is why this story is told here.

Such cases usually offer interesting bits of information which enable us to suggest a time and place for the case, and which add to our knowledge about the Sages.

Let us examine this incident: (a) The case is carried to the לשכת הגזית where the Sanhedrin used to meet at the Temple in Jerusalem. This proves that it happened before the destruction of the Temple. (b) There are several Rabban Gamliels in the history of the Sanhedrin. Often it is difficult to tell which Gamliel is meant in the text. Gamliel I, called the Elder, lived in Jerusalem. His grandson, Rabban Gamliel II, lived in Yavneh twenty years or so after the destruction. Obviously, the story concerns Gamliel I of Jerusalem.

What is more fascinating is the reply of Nahum, the Scribe. He traces the line of tradition for his opinion back to Moses at Sinai. This concept of הלכה למשה מסיני seems simple but it is not (see *Encyclopedia Talmudit*, 9: 365-387). It seems wise to interpret it as a reference to very old laws whose origins were lost in antiquity and were revered as if they had originated with Moses at Sinai. Students should compare the chain of tradition quoted here with that in *Avot*, Chapter I, to note the differences.

It is suggested that the class bring in reports on both Gamliel I, who was called גמליאל הזקן, and his grandson Gamliel II, who was called גמליאל דיבנה.

---

(7) **וחכמים אומרים**

Differences of opinion occur frequently among the Rabbis. Whenever one Sage is opposed by the חכמים, the final decision agrees with them.

---

(8) **מי שיש לו**

The class might discuss:

(a) Why should it be necessary to set such limitations upon who may and who may not accept לקט, שכחה, פאה?

(b) What is the difference between the American welfare system and the Jewish approach to the problem? Is there a welfare system in modern Israel? How does it work?

(c) Is the American welfare system succeeding? Why/Why not?

---

(9) **עזיבה**

The emphasis is upon the verb תעזוב. The landowner is not to give *pe'ah* to any particular poor man. He must leave it for the poor to take. The owner might give it to a poor relative and thus gain a direct or indirect benefit. That is forbidden. All the poor are to be treated equally.

---

(10)   כאילו בית המקדש קיים ומקריב קרבנות

The Rabbis of the Talmud looked back upon Temple times as the glorious age of Jewish history. There were many *mitzvot* associated with the sacrificial system. It was their cherished hope to live to see the Restoration and to observe those *mitzvot*. The thought that one might live to see the restored Temple and refuse the privilege of offering sacrifices was utterly scandalous. This indicates the high priority which they assigned to giving one's proper share in relieving distress. It lends itself to a full discussion of giving to the U.J.A. locally.

---

(11)   ביכורים

The sections on ביכורים and ראיון are included here because they add colorful elements to the religious practices of farmers in Israel. Requiring the farmer to bring ביכורים and ראיון to Jerusalem binds him closer to the Temple and to the centrality of Jerusalem.

The laws and procedures of ביכורים are to be read in *Devarim* 26: 1-11 and *Shemot* 23:19. The seven products subject to ביכורים are listed in *Devarim* 8:8.

The *mitzvah* of *Bikkurim* consists of two parts: *bringing* the produce to the Sanctuary, and *reciting the formula* acknowledging God's bounty. The formula recited by the pilgrim is among the oldest prayers in our liturgy. It should be read and translated fully. Its use on Passover should be discussed.

It is obvious from the text האדמה אשר נתת לי that only a landowner could recite the formula. His tenant, his messenger, or any other person forbidden to own property could not recite it. This raises the problem of the propertied proselyte who could not say אשר נשבע ה' לאבותינו.

This quotation is from the *Code* of Maimonides written in the 12th century. This became the dominant Jewish opinion. (In prayer, too, the proselyte acts like all Jews.)

---

(12)   אב המון גוים

This quotation contradicts the preceding paragraph. It is taken from the Jerusalem Talmud. Our classic sources disagree! Which becomes the law? Halakhic authorities did not agree about the answer.

(13) כיצד מעלין

This passage is too difficult in Hebrew. It should be read in the English translation, *Bikkurim* 3: 2-8.

---

(14) התקינו שיהיו

This experience parallels that of reciting ברכות for the Torah reading. Originally, every person read his own portion. But eventually not everyone could read. Appointing a professional reader only for those who could not read proved too embarrassing. Therefore, the professional was assigned to read for everyone called to the Torah.

---

(15) הראיון

The class should read *Devarim* 16:16, *Shemot* 23: 14-17, and *Shemot* 34:23. This is our first encounter with בית שמאי and בית הלל. Students probably will have learned stories and sayings of the two masters. It would be well to review what they have learned. Reports on the two Sages and their schools might be assigned (cf. A. H. Blumenthal, *If I Am Not For Myself: A Study of Hillel*, United Synagogue of America: 1973). This illustrates the general rule that in conflicts between בית שמאי and בית הלל the law usually follows בית הלל.

---

(16) כל זכורך

There are several categories in connection with the observance of any *mitzvah*. The two opposites are חייב i.e., obligated, and אסור i.e., forbidden. Then there are פטור i.e., exempt, e.g., a mourner before a funeral is exempt from prayer, an exemption which will soon pass; and finally, as we have here, שאינן חייבות i.e., not obligated (but not forbidden).

A woman is not obligated to observe the *mitzvah* of ראיון but she may observe it if she wishes to do so.

Americans define a slave as one who belongs totally to another. His master may give him a wife who may bear him children, but then the master may break up the family by selling each of them, including the parents, to separate masters. The slave has no rights of any kind.

Not so the Hebrew slave in the Bible and the Talmud. He is a person who, due to unfortunate circumstances, is condemned to serve a master for a limited period of time. His lot, in part, is due to his own action. He is not the object of pity as one caught in a web from which only others can extricate him. His lot is more comparable to that of the poor and other unfortunates.

The Talmud often speaks of such a slave as קנה אדון אחר. He went out of his way to acquire another lord, therefore he cannot truly serve the One and Only Lord. However, he shares with his master an obligation to obey the Torah, and when there is conflict between the property rights of the master and the religious obligations of the slave, the court forces the master to yield to the demands of the law. The master has no choice. He must yield.

This principle כופין אותו, forcing one of the parties to a conflict to do what he ought to do, occurs in other situations as well.

It is worth noting that the conflict between slave and master is concerned with the right of the slave to marry. In Judaism, every man is religiously obligated to marry and bear children.

Two further points about this last paragraph:

(a) Bet Hillel yields to Bet Shammai . . . an unusual situation.

(b) The decision to force the master to accept a note from the slave and to free him is derived not from a normal Rabbinic interpretation of a verse in the Bible. They often devised ethical concepts which they invoke when necessary. This is a new form of Rabbinic activity which we encounter for the first time. Here it is: מפני תקון העולם, which may be translated as "for the improvement of human society." It is invoked several times in the Mishnah (see *Gittin* 4:2ff), as is its companion injunction, מפני דרכי שלום. There are a number of such ethical maxims which enable the Rabbis to expand the application of the *halakhah*.

The Torah holds a special place in Jewish tradition as the revealed word of God. All *halakhah* is derived from it. Occasionally the Rabbis invoke a verse outside of the Torah to support or reaffirm the law.

The verse לא תהו בראה לשבת יצרה is not in the Torah. It is taken from *Yisha'yahu* 45:18. Students may read the full verse, which combines Creation with man's duty to populate the world. This method of going outside of the Torah for halakhic support is another demonstration of Rabbinic innovation.

CHAPTER FOUR: TEXTS
פרק רביעי: תלמוד תורה

ותלמוד תורה כנגד כולם

א.   אלו דברים שאין להם שעור: הפאה, והביכורים, והראיון, וגמילות חסדים, ותלמוד תורה. אלו דברים שאדם אוכל פירותיהם בעולם הזה והקרן קיימת לעולם הבא, ואילו הן: כבוד אב ואם, וגמילות חסדים, והשכמת בית המדרש שחרית וערבית, והכנסת אורחים, ובקור חולים, והכנסת כלה, ולוית המת, ועיון תפלה, והבאת שלום בין אדם לחבירו, ותלמוד תורה כנגד כולם (תוספתא פאה).[1]

ב.   1. גדול ת״ת יותר מבנין בית המקדש (מגילה ט״ז, ב).
     2. גדול ת״ת יותר מכבוד אב ואם (שם).
     3. גדול ת״ת יותר מהצלת נפשות (מגילה ט״ז, ב).
     4. גדול ת״ת מן הכהונה ומן המלכות (יומא ע״ב, ב).[2]

ג.   הלומד מחברו פרק אחד, או הלכה אחת, או פסוק אחד, או דבור אחד, או אפילו אות אחת צריך לנהוג בו כבוד (פרקי אבות ו, ג).[3]

ד.   היה רבי טרפון וזקנים מסובין בעלית בית נתזה בלוד, נשאלה שאילה זו בפניהם: תלמוד גדול או מעשה גדול. נענה רבי טרפון ואמר: מעשה גדול. נענה רבי עקיבא ואמר: תלמוד גדול. נענו כולם ואמרו תלמוד גדול שהתלמוד מביא לידי מעשה (קדושין מ, ב).[4]

וְלִמַּדְתֶּם אותם ושמרתם לעשותם (דברים ה, א).[5]

ה.   אף על פי שאמרו, האב חייב ללמד את בנו תורה, אפילו הכי, אם לא למדו אביו חייב הוא ללמד את עצמו שנאמר **ולמדתם אותם** (קדושין כ״ט, ב).

ו.   הוא ללמוד ובנו ללמד, הוא קודם לבנו (שם).

וְלִמַּדְתֶּם אותם את בניכם (דברים י״א, י״ט).[6]

ז.   מלמד שהאב חייב ללמד את בנו תורה (קידושין כ״ט, ב).

והודעתם לבניך ולבני בניך (דברים ד, ט).

ח.   לומר לך שכל המלמד את בנו תורה, מעלה עליו הכתוב כאילו למדו לו, ולבנו, ולבן בנו עד סוף כל הדורות (קדושין ל, א).

ט.   המלמד את בן חבירו תורה מעלה עליו הכתוב כאילו ילדו (סנהדרין י״ט, ב).

וְלִמַּדְתֶּם אותם את בניכם (דברים י״א, י״ט).

י.   אמר ר׳ יהודה אמר רב, זכור אותו האיש לטוב, ויהושע בן גמלא שמו, שאלמלא
     הוא נשתכח תורה מישראל. שבתחילה מי שיש לו אב מלמדו תורה ומי שאין לו אב
     לא היה לומד תורה, עד שבא ר׳ יהושע בן גמלא והתקין שיהיו מושיבין מלמדי
     תינוקות. ועל זה זכור הוא לטוב ... התקינו שיהיו מושיבין מלמדי תינוקות
     בירושלים, מאי דרוש? **כי מציון תצא תורה** (ישעיהו ב, ד). ועדיין מי שיש לו אב היה
     מעלו ומלמדו, ומי שאין לו אב לא היה עולה ולומד. התקינו שיהיו מושיבין בכל
     פלך ופלך ומכניסין אותו כבן ט״ז. מי שהיה רבו כועס עליו, מבעיט בו ויוצא. עד
     שבא ר׳ יהושע בן גמלא ותיקן שיהיו מושיבין מלמדי תינוקות בכל מדינה ומדינה,
     ובכל עיר ועיר, ומכניסין אותו כבן ו׳ וכבן ז׳ (בבא בתרא כ״א, א).[7]

**והיה אם שמוע תשמעו אל מצותי אשר אנכי מצוה אתכם היום לאהבה את ה׳
אלהיכם ולעבדו בכל לבבכם ובכל נפשכם** (דברים י״א, י״ג).

י״א. שמא תאמר, הרי למדתי תורה בשביל שאהיה עשיר, ובשביל שאקרא רבי, ובשביל
      שאקבל שכר, ת״ל **לאהבה את ה׳ אלהיכם** כל מה שאתם עושים לא תעשו אלא
      מאהבה (נדרים ס״ב, א). **ולעבדו** זה תלמוד ... אתה אומר זה תלמוד או אינו אלא
      עבודה ממש? כשהוא אומר **ויקח אלהים את האדם ויניחהו בגן עדן לעבדה
      ולשמרה** (בראשית ב, ט״ו). וכי מה עבודה לשעבר? ומה שמירה לשעבר? הא למדת,
      ולעבדו, זה תלמוד (ספרי, עקב, י״א, י״ג). דבר אחר **ולעבדו** זו תפילה ... או אינו
      אלא עבודה? ת״ל **בכל לבבך ובכל נפשך ובכל מאדך** (דברים ד, ה). וכי יש לך
      עבודה בלב? הא מה ת״ל **ולעבדו בכל לבבכם** זו תפילה (תענית ב, א).[8]

י״ב. אפילו לא שנה אדם אלא פרק אחד שחרית, ופרק אחד ערבית, קיים מצות **לא ימוש
      ספר התורה הזה מפיך** (יהושע א, ח). אמר רבי יוחנן משום רבי שמעון בן יוחאי
      אפילו לא קרא אדם קריאת שמע אלא שחרית וערבית, קיים **לא ימוש** (מנחות צ״ט,
      ב).[9]

י״ג. היה רבי מאיר אומר: מניין שאפילו גוי ועוסק בתורה שהוא ככהן גדול? שנאמר
      אשר יעשה אותם האדם וחי בהם (ויקרא י״ח, ה). כהנים, לויים ישראלים לא נאמר
      אלא **האדם**, הא למדת, שאפילו גוי עוסק בתורה הרי הוא ככהן גדול (סנהדרין כ״ט,
      א).[10]

וחי בהם

י״ד. מניין לפקוח נפש שדוחה את השבת. אמר ר׳ יהודה אמר שמואל: דכתיב, **ושמרתם
      את חקותי ואת משפטי אשר יעשה אותם האדם וחי בהם** (ויקרא י״ח, ה), ולא
      שימות בהם (יומא פ״ה, ב).[11]

37

ט״ו. אמר ר׳ יוחנן משום ר׳ שמעון בן יהוצדק: נמנו וגמרו בעליית בית נתזה בלוד, כל
עבירות שבתורה חוץ מעבודת כוכבים, וגלוי עריות, ושפיכת דמים. אם אומרים לו
לאדם עבור ולא תהרג, יעבר ואל יהרג ... שנאמר **וחי בהם** ולא שימות בהם
(סנהדרין ע״ד, א).[12]

ט״ז. הלל אומר: הוי מתלמידיו של אהרן, אוהב שלום, ורודף שלום, אוהב את הבריות
ומקרבן לתורה (אבות א, י״ב).

י״ז. שמאי אומר עשה תורתך קבע (שם, ט״ו).

י״ח. אמר רבא: כל תלמיד חכם שאין תוכו כברו אינו תלמיד חכם (יומא ע״ב, ב).

י״ט. אוי להם ... לתלמידי חכמים שעוסקין בתורה ואין בהם יראת שמים (שם).[13]

כ.   אני בריה וחברי בריה, אני מלאכתי בעיר, והוא מלאכתו בשדה. אני משכים
למלאכתי והוא משכים למלאכתו. כשם שהוא אינו מתגדר במלאכתי, כך אני איני
מתגדר במלאכתו. ושמא תאמר אני מרבה והוא ממעיט, שנינו, אחד המרבה ואחד
הממעיט ובלבד שכיון לבו לשמים (ברכות י״ז, א).

CHAPTER FOUR:
THE STUDY OF TORAH

This chapter is concerned with the *mitzvah* of Talmud Torah. It is not related to *Vayikra* 19. It is introduced here because of the Rabbinic statement in Chapter 3: ותלמוד תורה כנגד כולם. In effect, the Rabbis have said that if we had to select only one *mitzvah* to convey the essence of Judaism, it would have to be Talmud Torah, for everything else derives from it. This chapter will explore that judgment.

(1) אלו דברים

Our first paragraph should be familiar to the class. It is a variation of the first selection in our last chapter. Students should compare the two. This one also ends with the words, ותלמוד תורה כנגד כולם.

The highest compliment that the Rabbis could pay to a sacred text was to incorporate it in the *Siddur*, as they did with this passage. Students will supply other examples: the *Shema*, *Mi Khamokha*, *Ashray*, etc. At one time, the Ten Commandments also were recited daily during prayer. Since most Jews prayed regularly, the constant repetition of these verses and phrases saturated the minds of many generations of Jews with ideas and values which gave direction to Jewish living.

It is suggested that the class learn the distinction between מצות בין אדם למקום and מצות בין אדם לחבירו. They should separate the *mitzvot* in this paragraph into the two categories. What conclusion does one derive from the two lists which emerge?

(2) גדול ת״ת

Our first objective, at the outset of this chapter, is to establish the high priority which the Rabbis assigned to the *mitzvah* to study Torah. It is suggested that the Bible readings be postponed until later, and the teacher concentrate on paragraph (ב).

These four sentences are further evidence of the supreme importance attached to Talmud Torah. Members of the class may disagree and discussion should be lively. The teacher can grant that there may be some exaggeration, but there also may be a modern parallel.

In all the under-developed countries in our day, the most serious need (next to food) is literacy. No people can raise itself from backwardness until its war against illiteracy is won. Literacy brings skills which, in turn, bring productivity. In Judaism, ignorance of Torah is an intolerable form of illiteracy.

---

(3)   הלומד מחבירו

The esteem in which teachers are held creates an attitude within a community towards learning. Again we seem to be in the area of slight exaggeration, but it serves to emphasize the Rabbinic estimate of Talmud Torah. The Rabbis would never say that giving a single meal to a poor man is a great *mitzvah*. But they seem to imply it about teaching him one letter. Why?

---

(4)   ר׳ טרפון ור׳ עקיבא

This discussion between Rabbi Akiva and Rabbi Tarfon is significant because it leads to the same conclusion . . . the super-importance of Talmud Torah.

The teacher will note the location of the meeting at Lud, near contemporary Lod. Students may want to learn whether ancient Lud has been excavated and what has been learned about it.

Of course, the difference of opinion could not be solved for all time. For our purposes here, the emphasis is upon the supremacy of the *mitzvah* of Talmud Torah. However, the teacher may choose to introduce the statement of Rabbi Shimon (*Avot* 1:17) לא המדרש העיקר אלא המעשה, and conduct a class discussion. Members of the class may be assigned reports on Rabbi Akiba and Rabbi Tarfon.

This Rabbinic emphasis upon the primacy of the *mitzvah* of Talmud Torah has made a profound imprint upon the Jewish mind and upon world opinion concerning Jews. The late Dr. Robert M. Hutchins, past president of the University of Chicago and of the Fund for the Republic once said:

The greatest contribution the Jews have made to American life is the idea that learning is a form of worship. One hates to think what would have been the plight of American education if it had not been for Jewish scholars and students.

---

(5) ולמדתם אותם

All that we have studied in this chapter, so far, has served only one objective: to express the Rabbinic devotion to the study of Torah. It is time now to turn to the Biblical sources of the *mitzvah*.

The first of these texts serves as the introduction to the repetition of the Ten Commandments (*Devarim* 5: 1-5). The class should read this section with special attention to the three basic ideas it contains:

(a) The *mitzvot* are directed to adults, not to children.

(b) The whole purpose of the commandments is to teach man how to act according to the Law of God. A *mitzvah* remains meaningless if it is not translated into human conduct.

(c) Observing the *mitzvot* enables expression by Israel of its Covenant.

It might be well to have the class learn these words by heart: ולמדתם אותם ושמרתם לעשותם.

---

(6) את בניכם

The next sections to be read in the Torah are שמע - ואהבת (*Devarim* 6: 4-9) and the והיה אם שמע (*Devarim* 11: 13-20). There are several other *mitzvot* in these sections and only the teacher can determine how deeply the class can delve into these texts. However, the phrase ושננתם לבניך is very pertinent as are the words ולמדתם אותם את בניכם. They constitute the actual words commanding a parent to teach the Torah to his children. The next paragraphs extend the obligation to teach to include one's grandchildren and the children of others.

---

(7)   ר׳ יהושע בן גמלא

These stories of Rabbi Joshua ben Gamla indicate how a community accepted its responsibility for the education of its children. Rabbi Shimon ben Shetah usually is credited with inaugurating the system of public schools in Judea. This is based upon a terse comment in the Yerushalmi (*Ketubot* 8:11). This story about Joshua ben Gamla is much meatier. In all probability, both contributed to this important step. They lived at about the same time, circa two centuries before the destruction.

---

(8)   ולעבדו

This sentence in the והיה אם שמע should be compared with the ואהבת. The word ולעבדו is missing in the latter; therefore it must have a special meaning in its actual context. We are offered two alternative meanings for the word ולעבדו: "to study" or "to pray."

There is a slight difficulty about the text. Adam and Eve were sent to the Garden of Eden לעבדה ולשמרה. In those idyllic days, there was no such thing as work, וכי מה עבודה לשעבר. Therefore, the word עבודה had to mean something else.

To worship (עבודה) always meant to pray. It also meant to conduct the service in the Temple. Here, it acquired another meaning: to study. This is the source for Dr. Robert Hutchins' comment that Jews contributed to America the conviction that study is a form of worship.

Equating worship with study could have come to Judaism only from the Rabbis. As long as the Temple stood, the word עבודה meant worship in the Temple. The survival of Judaism under the Rabbis endowed the study of Torah with the highest of values, עבודה.

---

(9)   קיים לא ימוש

The source of all Rabbinic law is the Torah. Occasionally, however, the Rabbis invoke passages outside the Torah to reenforce a law or a thought.

The question is, granted the importance of the *mitzvah* to study Torah, how much Torah should one study each day to fulfill the *mitzvah*? They reformulate the *mitzvah* by using a phrase from *Yehoshu'a* 1:9. The class can read all the nine verses, noting that this has nothing to do with Jewish law. It is an exhortation to Joshua to lead the people to the promised land according to the laws of the Torah. Verse 9 is not directed to the Jewish people, only to Joshua.

This did not bother the Rabbis. They lifted the verse out of context and made it the focal point of the commandment to study Torah. And it sharpens the question. The phrase לא ימוש seems to imply that one must study all day, which is impossible.

The teacher should draw attention to the difference of opinion within our paragraph. One simply cannot set a uniform standard for all. The discussion, here, is concerned with the minimum standards. Utilizing the *Siddur*, the Rabbis have devised a method to enable every Jew to fulfill his obligation.

Students should turn to pp. 6-8 of *Sim Shalom*. This section contains a number of preliminary prayers recited by the worshipper every day. From the last paragraph on page 6 almost to the bottom of page 8 (before אלהי נשמה), one is concerned with the *mitzvah* of Talmud Torah. This page should be read carefully.

The worshipper recites a *berakhah* לעסוק בדברי תורה which he encounters nowhere else. He recites a second *berakhah*, praising God as המלמד תורה לעמו ישראל. He then recites the *berakhah* with which every Jew is familiar . . . אשר בחר בנו. In the synagogue, this *berakhah* always is followed by a reading from the Torah scroll. The worshipper, at this juncture, does not use a scroll, but he quotes from the Torah and he also adds another quotation from the Rabbinic literature. The *Birkat Kohanim* is a quotation from *Bemidbar* 8: 24-26, and the אלו דברים (which is our first quotation in this chapter) is taken from a mixed Rabbinic source. The worshipper, thus, has studied both Written and Oral Torah as part of his preliminary prayers.

The teacher should inform the class that these selections reflect the Ashkenazic practice. In other rites, there are variations. Rabbi Solomon Luria (1510-1578) substituted the following Biblical verses for the Priestly Benediction.

You shall not go up and down as a tale-bearer among your people; neither shall you stand idly by the blood of your neighbor; I am the Lord.

You shall not hate your brother in your heart; you shall surely rebuke your neighbor and not suffer sin because of him.

You shall not take vengeance nor bear any grudge against the children of your people, but you shall love your neighbor as yourself. I am the Lord (*Vayikra* 19: 16-18).

Since these verses are in *Vayikra* 19, they will be discussed in later chapters. The commentary in Hertz's *Daily Prayer Book* (p. 12-17) may be helpful to the teacher.

There are variations in the Rabbinic selection as well. The teacher might bring an Orthodox prayer book to class. De Sola Pool's *RCA Prayer Book*, Hertz's *Daily Prayer Book*, or Birnbaum's *Prayer Book* are good examples. They contain many more pages of Biblical and Rabbinic literature to be recited by worshippers every day.

It is advisable for the class to discuss whether varying the Biblical and Rabbinic quotations is a desirable thing to introduce in planning Conservative services for adults or for young people.

The suggestion that the study of any chapter or one paragraph a day fulfills the commandment may be passed on to the class. The class might select a book of the Bible to be read in this manner by those who wish to participate in the project.

---

(10)   גוי עוסק בתורה

Rabbi Meir's dictum is another emphasis upon the value of Talmud Torah. The proof text is *Vayikra* 18:5 and the class should read verses 1-5.

The Torah frequently expresses its horror of the pagan immorality of the people with whom the Israelites came into contact. Therefore, a non-Jew who studies Torah and adheres to its moral principles is the equal of the High Priest.

Rabbi Meir derives his lesson from the word אדם, the name used for the Biblical ancestor of all mankind. Any one who rejects paganism and obeys the law of the Torah thereby demonstrates his goodness and his decency. The contrast in Rabbi Meir's statement is not between Jew and non-Jew, but between the demands of the Torah and the pagan practices that preceded the Torah.

To understand this innovation, we must define paganism. The Torah brought a new outlook into the behavior required of man. The rest of Chapter 18 is devoted to a description of incest, forbidden blood and familial marriages. Other abominable sexual practices also are forbidden and it becomes obvious, by reading all of Chapter 18, that there were no such restrictions among pagan peoples. The Canaanites, who were driven out of the promised land to make way for the children of Israel, were guilty of all of these paganisms.

Further description of paganism is given in *Devarim* 18: 9-14. The class will not be able to read it all in Hebrew, but the full meaning of the section should be reviewed in English. This, after all, is the difference between Judaism and its predecessor religions. *Devarim* 23:18 (use the new JPS translation) refers to Temple prostitutes both male and female. The class might be assigned to research "Moloch worship," the burning or sacrifice of children by fire. The *Jewish Encyclopedia* and *Encyclopedia Judaica* have good articles.

The Torah attempts to eliminate paganism from the world by substituting new moral and worship patterns. Rabbi Meir makes acceptance of these changes available to Jew and non-Jew alike.

---

(11) ולא שימות בהן

The ingenuity of Rabbi Meir in deriving so vital a message from the one word, אדם, is matched by the genius of Rabbi Samuel, quoted by Rabbi Judah, in finding an equally profound lesson in the two words which follow וחי בהם. Sometimes the demands of one *mitzvah* contradict the requirements of another. For example, it is a *mitzvah* for me to save a man whose life is threatened. On the other hand, it is forbidden for me to fire a rifle on the Shabbat. If I see a wild bear chasing a man, may I use the rifle to save him?

The question is not what do you or I think, but what does the law require? We must remember that the prohibition against firing the rifle, in the minds of the Rabbis, originates with God! We have no way of knowing His purposes. To substitute our judgement for His is presumptuous.

Rabbi Samuel resolves the conflict by interpreting the two words וחי בהם. They are superfluous. The sentence is complete without them. If God inserted them into the text, He meant us to derive some wisdom from them. Rabbi Samuel informs us that the purpose of observing the Torah is to enable man to live, וחי בהם ולא שימות בהם, and not to die for it.

45

This is a very complicated problem and the Rabbis engaged in considerable discussion about it. But the principle is established, ולא שימות בהם, and it is applied widely. Here, however, it is limited to violating the Shabbat.

---

(12) יעבור ואל יהרג

Beginning with the second century B.C.E. when the Greeks sought to force Jews to violate their laws, the question arose whether one might disobey the law to save his life. This problem occurred during the Holocaust as well. There were many Hassidic Jews in the ghettos and camps whose Rabbis were with them and whenever a problem occurred which involved violating the law, the Hassidim always consulted their Rabbis. Books have been written about these experiences (in Hebrew, ממעמקים in three volumes by Rav Oshri and in English, *The Holocaust and Halakhah* by Rabbi Irving Rosenbaum). The teacher may wish to bring typical cases to the class for discussion.

Our paragraph permits the violation of all laws, with the exception of three. This may lead to a discussion about the occasions when one is called upon to risk one's life. Tell the Hanukkah story of Hannah and her seven sons and any other story of such martyrdom. Are there any situations that the class can think of in which they would risk their lives? To save a parent, brother or sister, any other loved one? Does the government have the right to draft people and send them to war to defend our shores?

---

(13) יראת שמים

In describing the ark to be built for the Tabernacle, the Torah (*Shemot* 25:11) requires that both the inside and the outside of the ark be covered with gold. This became a symbolic expression for a person of integrity who is the same inwardly as he is outwardly. Pride and arrogance are especially deplorable among teachers. Both the scholar and the student are to be judged by their conduct, by the influence which the study of Torah exerts upon them. These paragraphs deal with this problem. The last paragraph is a general summary of the Rabbis' attitude towards all men.

CHAPTER FIVE: TEXTS
פרק חמישי: חמס

א. **לא תגנב** (שמות כ, י״ג).[1]

בגונב נפשות הכתוב מדבר. אתה אומר בגונב נפשות, או אינו אלא בגונב ממון? אמרת, צא ולמד משלש עשרה מדות שהתורה נדרשת בהן, דבר הלמד מעניינו. במה הכתוב מדבר, בנפשות, אף כאן בנפשות (סנהדרין פ״ו, א).

ב. **לא תגנובו** (ויקרא י״ט, א).

בגונב ממון הכתוב מדבר. אתה אומר: בגונב ממון או אינו אלא בגונב נפשות? אמרת, צא ולמד משלש עשרה מדות שהתורה נדרשת בהן, דבר הלמד מעניינו. במה הכתוב מדבר, בממון, אף כאן בממון (שם).

ג. שבעה גנבים הם, הראשון שבגנבים גונב דעת בני אדם (מכילתא משפטים).[2]

ד. הגנב פסול לעדות (הרמב״ם, הלכות עדות, י, סעיף ד).[3]

ה. **כי מלאה הארץ חמס** (בראשית ו, ג).

א״ר לוי: חמס, זה עבודת אלילים. חמס, זה גילוי עריות. חמס, זה שפיכות דמים (בראשית רבה, ל״א).

ו. **ותמלא הארץ חמס.**

א״ר יוחנן: בא וראה כמה גדול כחה של חמס. שהרי דור המבול עברו על הכל ולא נחתם עליהם גזר דינם עד שפשטו ידיהם בגזל, שנאמר, **כי מלאה הארץ חמס** (סנהדרין ק״ח, א). איזה חמס ואיזה גזל? א״ר חנינא: חמס, שאינה שווה פרוטה, וגזל ששווה פרוטה. וכך היו אנשי דור המבול עושים. היה אחד מהם מוציא קופתו מלאה תרמוסים, והיה זה בא ונוטל פחות משווה פרוטה. וזה בא ונוטל פחות משווה פרוטה עד מקום שאין יכול להוציאן ממנו בדין (בראשית רבה ל״א).[4]

ז. שאלו תלמידיו את רבן יוחנן בן זכאי: מפני מה החמירה תורה בגנב יותר מגזלן? אמר להם: זה השווה כבוד עבד לכבוד קונו, וזה שלא השווה כבוד עבד לכבוד קונו. כביכול: עשה עין של מטה כאילו אינו רואה, ואוזן של מטה כאילו אינה שומעת . . . ויאמרו **לא יראה יה ולא יבין אלהי יעקב** (תהלים צ״ד, ז) (בבא קמא ע״ט, א).[5]

ח. **לא תגנובו, ולא תכחשו, ולא תשבעו** (ויקרא י״ט, י״א). אם גנבת, סופך לכחש, סופך לשקר, סופך לשבע לשקר (ספרא קדושים י״ט, י״א).

ט.   מצווה גוררת מצווה (אבות ד, ב).

י.   עבירה גוררת עבירה (שם).[6]

י"א.   **לא תשבעו בשמי לשקר וחללת את שם אלהיך** (ויקרא י"ט, י"ב). מה ת"ל? לפי
        שנאמר **לא תשא את שם ה' אלהיך לשוא** (שמות כ, ז). יכול אין חייבים אלא על שם
        המיוחד בלבד. מניין לרבות את כל הכנויים? ת"ל **לא תשבעו בשמי**, כל שם שיש לי
        (תורת כהנים).

י"ב.   **לא תלין פעולת שכיר אתך עד בוקר** (ויקרא י"ט, י"ג).
        אחד שכר אדם, ואחד שכר בהמה, ואחד שכר כלים, יש בו משום **לא תלין פעולת
        שכיר.** ואמר קרא **לא תלין פעולת שכיר,** כל שפעולתו אתך (בבא מציעא קי"א, ב).[7]

י"ג.   **לא תקלל חרש** (ויקרא י"ט, י"ד).
        אין לי אלא חרש. מניין לרבות כל אדם? ת"ל **בעמך לא תאר** (שמות כ"ב, כ"ז) (תורת
        כהנים).
        לא תקלל חרש— באומללים שבעמך הכתוב מדבר (סנהדרין ס"ד, ב).[8]

י"ד.   **לפני עוור לא תתן מכשול** (שם).
        מה הוא **ולפני עוור . . .** ? לפני סומא בדבר. היה נוטל ממך עצה אל תתן לו עצה
        שאינה הגונה לו (איכה רבתי ג).

ט"ו.   **לפני עוור לא תתן מכשול.**
        רבי נתן אומר: מניין שלא יושיט אדם כוס יין לנזיר ואבר מן החי לבן נח? ת"ל, **לפני
        עוור לא תתן מכשול** (פסחים כ"ב, ב).

ט"ז.   **לפני עוור לא תתן מכשול.**
        במכה בנו הגדול הכתוב מדבר (מועד קטן י"ז, א).

י"ז.   **לפני עוור לא תתן מכשול.**
        אמר רב יהודה אמר רב: כל המלווה מעות שלא בעדים, עובר משום **ולפני עוור לא
        תתן מכשול** (בבא מציעא ע"ה, ב).[9]

י"ח.   **ויראת מאלהיך אני ה'** (שם).
        דבר המסור ללב נאמר בו **ויראת מאלהיך** (קידושין ל"ב, ב).

48

CHAPTER FIVE: SOCIAL VIOLENCE

(1)   לא תגנב/תגנובו

Students will be familiar with the prohibition from the Ten Commandments against stealing. They should compare the formulation here in *Vayikra* with the two versions of the Ten Commandments (*Shemot* 20:13 and *Devarim* 5:17). They will speedily note that our verse here, in *Vayikra*, is in the plural while the others are in the singular. To the Rabbinic mind, such variation is not accidental. It is a deliberate act by God to convey something special. Our first sections (א) and (ב) indicate their opinions of the difference between לא תגנב and לא תגנובו. In making their explanation, they reveal one of the methods which they employed in interpreting and expanding the law of the Torah.

Students should turn back to Chapter 2 to reread Rabbi Akiba's method of attaching special meaning to the words את and אך. However, this method was one which Rabbi Ishmael rejected. Thus there were some rules of interpretation about which the Rabbis differed. But there were other rules which were adopted unanimously. The number of such regulations about which there was total agreement was 13. Each is called *midah* a method or interpretation, and the Hebrew expression is שלש עשרה מידות שהתורה נדרשת בהן (thirteen methods by which the Torah is interpreted). They are numbered and always are recited in the same order.

The one which the Rabbis utilize here is number 12. It is called דבר הלמד מעניינו, "a law which is derived from the context in which it appears." We are not certain about the origin of these 13 *midot*. Tradition tells us that seven of them were fashioned by Hillel, and six more were added by Rabbi Ishmael. Our *midah* is among Hillel's original seven.

In the commandments, לא תגנב is preceded by two laws, לא תרצח and לא תנאף both of which were punishable by death. The third law, לא תגנב, which also is in the singular must, therefore, carry the same penalty. Only the theft of a person, kidnaping, demands this penalty.

On the other hand, לא תגנובו (*Vayikra* 19:11) is followed by other offenses stated in the plural for which the penalty is not death. Therefore, like them, it requires only monetary compensation.

The teacher might want the class to learn the phrases שלש עשרה מידות דבר הלמד מעניינו and שהתורה נדרשת בהן by heart.

---

(2) גנבת דעת

Another form of גנבה is called גנבת דעת, "the stealing of the mind." It is not concerned so much with the theft of material things as with the deception and insincerity which we frequently practice on one another. The students should read *II Shmu'el* 15: 1-6, the story of Absalom's attempt to ingratiate himself with the Israelites. The Bible says of it ויגנב אבשלום את לב אנשי ישראל. When Laban overtook Jacob, he accused him with the same words: ותגנב את לבבי (*Bereshit* 31:16).

In Rabbinic literature גנבת לב is called גנבת דעת, "to steal the mind." It means to deceive, deliberately to mislead, to give bad advice, to promise things that one does not intend to fulfill. Even to invite someone to dinner knowing that he cannot accept is גנבת דעת because it is an insincere expression of hospitality. There does not have to be any monetary loss involved in גנבת דעת. The Rabbis insist, however, that worse than all the other thieves is the one who is guilty of גנבת דעת.

This is an opportunity to explore a number of issues on the contemporary scene and to ask whether they constitute גנבת דעת. How about advertising, in general? Using beautiful women in TV ads for cars? An actor putting his reputation behind a brand of coffee or a bottle of wine or some other commercial product? Does the fact that he gets paid for what he does constitute moral justification? Is a politician who promises everything to everybody guilty of גנבת דעת? Is a teacher who is improperly prepared for a class just as guilty? What about people who have been seduced into various religious cults? The students are old enough to make suggestions of their own as to what constitutes גנבת דעת.

This is an excellent opportunity to introduce the fact that Jews live by values which originate in two civilizations, American and Judaism. In American law, the purchase of any object is based on the rule of *caveat emptor*, "let the buyer beware." It is up to the purchaser to know what he is buying. In

Judaism, the governing principle is גנבת דעת. The seller "steals the mind" of the purchaser by failing to disclose any defect in the object at hand.

---

(3)   פסול לעדות

Our sentence, הגנב פסול לעדות, is another illustration of a contradiction between two civilizations. In Judaism, the purpose of a court procedure is to determine the truth and to arrive at a just decision. A thief who has no regard for the truth will not contribute to the total purpose of the court. Therefore he may not testify.

The American system begins with the constitutional rights of the individual. Though everyone may know that the defendant is guilty, it is possible for him to be discharged because of some violation of his rights.

The American system, like the European system, had to wrestle with the problems of the rights of monarchies and aristocracies who claimed a "divine right of kings." This conflict produced many great wars and many magnificent documents such as the Magna Carta and the American Declaration of Independence.

Jewish monarchies, on the other hand, were confronted with Prophets and Rabbis who spoke in the name of God, the Author of the whole system of Jewish thought. They began with God's Creation of the world, His requirements of justice and righteousness, His giving of the Law, and His setting of a goal for the whole of humanity. Even the king is made subservient to this Biblical law. (The class should carefully read *Devarim* 17: 15-20.) In very large measure, this explains most of the differences between Western and Jewish goals for humanity.

Once the class grasps the difference, it should engage in vigorous debate about the two value systems.

---

(4)   חמס

One of the stories of the Torah which fails to furnish us with adequate detail is that of the Flood. What sins had the generation of the Flood committed to warrant its total destruction? The Torah does not tell us. It says merely כי מלאה הארץ חמס. The word חמס occurs only three times in the Torah and its

51

meaning is uncertain. In 1917, the first Jewish translation of the Bible into English was made by a group of scholars. It translated the word חמס as "violence." In 1962, a revised Jewish translation of the Torah was made and it translates חמס as "injustice." Which is it?

The Rabbis were perplexed by the same problem. What sins could possibly provoke God to destroy mankind? They offered a variety of definitions of the word חמס. These include murder, incest and idolatry. Paragraph (ה) accepts the usual definition of חמס as violence. Paragraph (ו) however offers a unique interpretation. In it, חמס is defined as something totally worthless, as valued at less than the smallest coin, שווה פרוטה.

The two opposite meanings of the word חמס point to the great versatility of the Rabbis. Though they respected the text, they often saw in it suggestions and meanings which were not on the surface.

Are sin and goodness readily identifiable? Is it easy to judge the character of our society? A community can be evil even if its sins are comparatively minor and petty. Goodness is a striving for perfection, and where that is missing or inadequate, the goal remains unattained. That is why Rabbi Yohanan has recourse to his exaggerated definition of חמס. A community of righteous people is totally committed to the search for the right. It may be unattainable, but it is the ever-present goal. This difference of opinion between these two sages reflects the varying goals which motivated their lives.

---

(5) הגנב והגזלן

The Torah uses two different words to describe a thief, גנב and גזלן. The difference between them is that the גנב steals furtively. He enters the home of his victim when the latter is away, fearing to be caught in the act. The גזלן has no such fear. He enters boldly and forcefully and is not afraid of his victims.

In setting forth the punishment and the compensation which are to be paid by the thief who is apprehended, the גנב is fined twice as much as the גזלן (*Shemot* 21:37, *Vayikra* 5:23). This naturally excited the curiosity of the students of Rabbi Yohanan ben Zakkai. The Rabbi drew a distinction between the two offenders. The Author of the prohibition against stealing is God. Neither thief is afraid of God's law. They both violate it. But the גזלן is not afraid of man either. He treats both God and man alike. The גנב, on the other hand, displays more fear of man than of God! God is the Master of the Universe and every one of us is His slave or servant. The גנב demonstrates more fear for the slave than for the Master. This makes his offense worse. The use of the word *mattah* is a substitute for God who, according to the Rabbis, sees and hears everything on earth.

---

(6) גוררת

The Rabbis never missed an opportunity to teach the cumulative effect of human conduct. As man's life evolves, the pattern of the values which he cherishes is determined by small decisions made early in life which he repeats and expands from time to time. Often, it takes only one cigarette to start smoking, or one act of charity to encourage another. The class might learn by heart the phrases עבירה גוררת עבירה and מצוה גוררת מצוה.

---

(7) לא תשבעו בשמי . . . לא תלין פעולת שכיר אתך

Both these paragraphs demonstrate one method employed by the Rabbis in elaborating the law. It seems to be a play upon words—words which seem to be unnecessary. In (י"א) the sentence would be complete if it read לא תשבעו לשקר. How else does one swear except by the Name of God? The word בשמי seems superfluous. In (י"ב) the word אתך falls into the same category. It is unnecessary. Such extra words provide the Rabbis with both the need and the opportunity to do something with them to expand the law.

---

(8) מניין לרבות

A deaf person cannot hear what one says to him or about him. Why, then, is it forbidden to curse him? In *Shemot* 22:27, which the class should read, the Torah prohibits the cursing of God and of rulers and princes. That, of course, helps to maintain peace within the community.

But what good is gained by prohibiting the cursing of the deaf? The Rabbis extricate themselves from this problem by elevating this meaningless prohibition to a value judgment, establishing an attitude towards all unfortunate people.

The verse in *Shemot* contains the sentence "You shall not revile God, nor curse a ruler of your people." Good Hebrew grammar requires the presence of the word בעמך "among your people." But not the Rabbis. They prefer to ignore the word "*nasi,*" and that leaves them with the sentence, "among your people you shall not curse."

---

(9)   לפני עוור

The Bible often is frustrating for those of us who study it. We have read only a few verses in *Vayikra* and the variety of material is profound. Sometimes it is difficult to tell whether we are dealing with the law to guide the community or with the ethical suggestions to guide the individual.

What kind of sentence is לפני עוור לא תתן מכשול? Fortunately, the Rabbis often come to our rescue. Their comments on לפני עוור לא תתן מכשול are truly inspiring.

The teacher should encourage the students to devise their own interpretations of this sentence.

CHAPTER SIX: TEXTS
פרק שישי: דבור

א. **לא תשא פני דל (ויקרא י"ט, ט"ו).**
שלא תאמר: עני הוא זה, והואיל ושאני והעשיר הזה חייבים לפרנסו, אזכנו, ונמצא
מתפרנס בנקיות. לכן נאמר, **לא תשא פני דל** (תורת כהנים ד, ב).

ב. **ולא תהדר פני גדול (שם).**
שלא תאמר: עשיר הוא זה, בן גדולים הוא, ואיך אביישנו? לכן נאמר, **לא תהדר פני
גדול** (שם ג).

ג. **בצדק תשפט עמיתך (שם).**
שלא יהא אחד יושב ואחד עומד; אחד מדבר כל צרכו, ואחד אומר לו קצור דבריך
(שבועות ל"ג, א).

ד. יהודה בן טבאי אומר . . . כשיהיו בעלי הדין עומדים לפניך, יהיו בעיניך כרשעים,
וכשנפטרים מלפניך יהיו בעיניך כזכאין (אבות א, ח).

ה. **לא תלך רכיל (ויקרא י"ט, ט"ז).**
תנא ר' ישמעאל: זה רכילות, זה לשון הרע (ירושלמי פאה פ"א, ה"א).

ו. **לא תלך רכיל.**
אמר ר' יוחנן משום רבי יוסף בן זמרא: כל המספר לשון הרע כאילו כופר בעיקר
(ערכין ט"ו, ב).

ז. **לא תלך רכיל.**
אמר רב חסדא, אמר מר עוקבא: כל המספר לשון הרע, אמר הקב"ה אין אני והוא
יכולים לדור בעולם (שם).

ח. **לא תלך רכיל.**
ארבעה דברים שהן נפרעים מן האדם בעולם הזה, והקרן קיימת לו לעולם הבא.
ואלו הם עבודה זרה, גלוי עריות, ושפיכת דמים. ולשון הרע כנגד כולם (ירושלמי
פאה א, א).

ט. **לא תלך רכיל.**
כל המספר לשון הרע אין לו חלק לעולם הבא (פרקי דרבי אליעזר נ"ג).

י. **לא תלך רכיל.**
ת״ר מניין לכשיצא לא יאמר אני מזכה וחבירי מחייבין אבל מה אעשה שחבירי רבו
עלי, ת״ל **לא תלך רכיל** (סנהדרין כ״ט, א).

י״א. **לא תעמוד על דם רעך** (שם).[6]
מניין לרודף אחרי חבירו להרגו, שניתן להצילו בנפשו? ת״ל **לא תעמוד על דם רעך**
(סנהדרין ע״ג, א).

י״ב. **לא תעמוד על דם רעך.**
מניין לרואה את חבירו טובע בנהר, או חיה גוררתו, או לסטין באין עליו, שהוא
חייב להצילו? ת״ל **לא תעמוד על דם רעך** (שם).

י״ג. **לא תעמוד על דם רעך.**
מניין שאם אתה יודע עדות לחברך שאי אתה רשאי לשתוק? ת״ל **לא תעמוד על דם
רעך** (תורת כהנים ד, ח).

י״ד. **הוכח תוכיח את עמיתך** (ויקרא י״ט, י״ז).[7]
אמר רבי טרפון: תמהני אני אם יש בדור הזה שמקבל תוכחה (ערכין ט״ז, א).

ט״ו. **הוכח תוכיח את עמיתך.**
אמר רבי אלעזר בן עזריה: תמיהני אני אם יש בדור הזה שיודע להוכיח (שם).

ט״ז. **הוכח תוכיח את עמיתך.**
כשם שמצווה על אדם לומר דבר הנשמע, כך מצווה על אדם שלא לומר דבר שאינו
נשמע (יבמות ס״ה, ב).

י״ז. **ואהבת לרעך כמוך** (ויקרא י״ט, י״ח).
אמר רבי עקיבא, זה כלל גדול בתורה. בן עזאי אומר: **זה ספר תולדות אדם**
(בראשית ה, א), זה כלל גדול בתורה (בראשית רבה כ״ד).[8]

י״ח. **ואהבת לרעך כמוך.**
אמר רב יהודה אמר רב: אסור לאדם לקדש אשה עד שיראנה, שמא ימצא בה דבר
מגונה, ותתגנה עליו. שנאמר, **ואהבת לרעך כמוך** (קדושין מ״א, א).[9]

י״ט. **ואהבת לרעך כמוך.**
ועוד אמר רבי מאיר: פותחים לו מן הפסוק שבתורה, ואומרים לו אילו היית יודע
שאתה עובר על **לא תקום** ועל **לא תטור** (ויקרא י״ט, י״ח), ועל **לא תשנא את אחיך
בלבבך** (ויקרא י״ט, י״ז), **ואהבת לרעך כמוך, וחי אחיך עמך** (ויקרא כ״ה, ל״ו); שמא
יעני ואין אתה יכול לפרנסו? אמר אילו הייתי יודע שהוא כן, לא הייתי נודר. הרי זה
מותר (נדרים פרק ט, ד).[10]

כ. **לא תקום ולא תטור** (ויקרא י״ט, י״ח).
איזו היא נקימה ואיזו היא נטירה? אמר לו השאילני מגלך. אמר לו לאו. למחר אמר
לו השאילני קרדומך. אמר לו איני משאילך כדרך שלא השאלתני. זו היא נקמה.

ואיזו היא נטירה? אמר לו השאילני קרדומך. אמר לו לאו. למחר אמר לו השאילני
מגלך. אמר לו הא לך, איני כמותך, שלא השאלתני. זו היא נטירה (יומא כ״ג, א).

CHAPTER SIX
THE POWER OF WORDS

(1)   **לא תשא ... לא תהדר**

On what basis should one judge the merits of a civilization? Some scholars would measure the freedom, the economic security, the level of education, the opportunities for personal growth, etc. enjoyed by the inhabitants in the community. While all of these criteria are very important, and no totalitarian regime can afford to extend these privileges to its people, Judaism seems to cherish another virtue above all others: the equality of all men before the law. We should note that such equality is far from universal. Our country fought a frightful Civil War over the issue, and the problem probably ranks first among the unattained goals of mankind.

There are codes of law which are older than the Torah. They contain condemnations of thievery, adultery, etc. which one would expect in any proposed system of human conduct, but none of them issues a call for full equality before the law. The class might discuss why this is so. Why didn't earlier codes demand or legislate such equality? The Torah was the first to consider rich and poor, strong and weak as equals in the pursuit of justice. The statement by Rabbi Judah ben Tabbai that both litigants should be viewed as wicked before the trial begins, and both as innocent after the verdict is rendered, leaves no room for partiality.

The first two paragraphs demonstrate how easy it is to rationalize a violation of the law. The motives invoked are of the purest: to save the poor man from dependence upon charity, to preserve the dignity and the status of the honorable man. It even acknowledges the duty of both the judge and the man of means to sustain the poor.

Nevertheless, it may not be done. Each *mitzvah*, maintaining strict equality before the court and sustaining the unfortunate, is to be kept and observed separately.

צדק (2)

The word צדק is a word which is unique. It seems to imply "the pursuit of perfection" (*Devarim* 16:20). If we are discussing justice, it demands perfect justice (*Devarim* 1:16, 16:18). If we are discussing weights and measures used by the merchant, it demands absolutely perfect instruments (*Vayikra* 19:36). The class should read all these references to acquire the flavor of the word צדק. Whether one of the litigants sits while the other stands seems of little consequence, except that it is a mild discrimination and that destroys the call for צדק. The word צדק really should be translated as "righteous."

לא תלך רכיל (3)

The word רוכל means a peddlar, and the verse cautions against imitating the peddlar who buys things in one household and sells them in another, or conveys bits of gossip from one group of people to another as he moves along. So it is with the man who transmits לשון הרע from one home to another. לשון הרע is condemned even when spoken by the most exalted of beings and for the loftiest purposes.

The class should read *Bereshit* 18: 9-14. This is the story of the angels predicting the birth of Isaac to Abraham. Sarah laughs at the news because, as she says, ואדוני זקן. But when God reports her laughter to Abraham, He has her say ואני זקנתי. God's purpose is to keep peace between Abraham and Sarah, but it nevertheless is regretted by the Torah. The Talmud calls God's change of words אבק לשון הרע.

זה לשון הרע (4)

One of the unique elements of the Torah is the way its contents are arranged. Some of the verses are part of the legal code, others are part of the historical record of Israel and its folklore literature. Still others are pure ethics or morals. And they are all in a jumble with little, if any, logical arrangement.

On the other hand, there are statements in the Torah that baffle us. The class should read the first half of *Vayikra* 19:16: לא תלך רכיל. It seems to be nothing more than a simple bit of moral exhortation. What makes it important?

To the Rabbis, every word in the Torah was a direct utterance from God filled with high significance and it was their function to try to discover what God wished to convey when He uttered these words. Surely God would not bother with such elementary advice as לא תלך רכיל. When Rabbi Ishmael identified לא תלך רכיל with לשון הרע, he removed it from the realm of the harmless or mischievous to the area of serious transgression of God's law. This leads other Rabbis to view the matter even more seriously. In all of these comments by the Rabbis, and, of course, there are many more, one witnesses their capacity to interpret the Biblical text with profound skill.

---

(5) ולשון הרע כנגד כולם

This paragraph which lists the three worst sins in the judgment of the Rabbis—idolatry, incest and murder—informs us that only לשון הרע exceeds them in wickedness. This arrangement reminds us of the listing of good deeds which culminates in the phrase ותלמוד תורה כנגד כולם. The class should review this.

---

(6) לא תעמד על דם רעך

The second half of *Vayikra* 19:16 is another one of these Biblical phrases which the Rabbis interpret with unusual skill. Every human being, they tell us, has a responsibility to every other human being. We are involved with each other and we have a responsibility to preserve and protect each other from all kinds of harm.

The teacher should point out the wide variety of cases which the Rabbis read into the prohibition of לא תעמד על דם רעך. We are responsible to save each other's lives and even to give testimony in court for our fellow men.

This is a complete negation of the modern tendency to avoid getting involved with others. It is one of the boldest affirmations of all Western religions. While Judaism has some attractive things to say about reward and punishment after death, it focuses man's purpose on earth upon his fellow men.

The class should discuss the philosophy of getting involved in terms of other Biblical and Rabbinic teachings which they have acquired.

---

(7) הוכח תוכיח

This is the first (and probably the last) time that we encounter a *mitzvah* which the Rabbis declare to be impossible to observe. It requires us to rebuke or to correct each other when we are guilty of wrong-doing. But it must be done with kindness and graciousness and without any ulterior motive or satisfaction derived from the act.

Rabbi Tarfon and Rabbi Elazar ben Azariah were contemporaries of Rabbi Akiba. They all suffered through the aftermath of the destruction of the Temple and the Hadrianic persecution. This may account for their pessimism.

---

(8) ר"ע ובן עזאי

ואהבת לרעך כמוך is one of the most popular verses in the entire Bible. Rabbi Akiba considers it to be the most meaningful verse in the whole Scripture. However, Ben Azzai sees a difficult problem. Who is this neighbor whom we are commanded to love as ourselves? Nobody will object to loving his neighbor, but he will exclude people of other races, creeds and colors from the category of "neighbor." Even the Nazis could have embraced ואהבת לרעך כמוך.

Ben Azzai therefore proposes that all of the verse in *Bereshit* 5:1 which culminates in בדמות אלהים עשה אותו is far more important. It affirms, without reservation, that every human being is made in the image of God.

The class should read the first two verses of *Bereshit* 5 to make certain of the point which Ben Azzai makes.

---

(9) אסור לקדש

Though the Rabbis interpreted the Bible as they found it, they really were primarily concerned with the law and with solutions to problems which arose. They kept looking for legal answers in the Bible text. Often these were not available, and under such circumstances, they had to resort to more general and even unrelated verses. For example, what does ואהבת לרעך כמוך have to do with whom one chooses for a bride? Absolutely nothing! Except that all of us are commanded to love each other, and if a man does not see his bride before he betrothes her, he may find her distasteful and end up violating the law of loving his neighbor. The relationship is very slim, but it serves the purpose.

60

(10)   ואהבת לרעך כמוך

This paragraph is another illustration of how the Rabbis used ואהבת לרעך כמוך, together with other general statements, to arrive at a legal decision.

In Biblical and Rabbinic times, men used to make all kinds of vows, some of which were designed to be guarantees of contributions to the Temple and others which were the result of careless or angry conversation. One man might say to another, "I vow that I will never talk to you again for the rest of my life."

The only way to cancel such foolish vows was to discuss the matter with a scholar who was permitted to cancel the oath. Rabbi Meir indicates how the scholar might approach the problem. He would ask a number of questions and if the answers were right, he would absolve the vow.

Again, there is no relationship between the questions and the vows but they cause the person to violate a number of general *mitzvot*, which, of course, may not be done. The verses quoted are: *Vayikra* 19:17, 18 and 25:36.

פרק שביעי: הזקן והגר

א. **מפני שיבה תקום** (ויקרא י״ט, ל״ב).[1]
יכול אפילו זקן אשמאי? ת״ל זקן. ואין זקן אלא חכם . . . רבי יוסי הגלילי אומר: אין
זקן אלא מי שקנה חכמה . . . רבי שמעון בן אלעזר אומר: מניין לזקן שלא יטריח?
ת״ל **זקן** . . . **ויראת**. איסי בן יהודה אומר: **מפני שיבה תקום** אפילו כל שיבה. אמר
רבי יוחנן, הלכה כאיסי בן יהודה (קידושין ל״ב, ב).[2]

ב. אמר רבי אלעזר: כל תלמיד חכם שאינו עומד מפני רבו, נקרא רשע (קידושין ל״ב,
ב).[3]

ג. **והדרת פני זקן** (שם).
חכם שנתמנה מוחלין לו על כל עונותיו. מאי טעמא, דכתיב, **והדרת פני זקן** וכתיב
בתריה **וכי יגור אתך גר** (ויקרא י״ט, ל״ג). מה גר מוחלין לו על כל עונותיו, אף חכם
שנתמנה מוחלין לו על כל עונותיו (ירושלמי, בכורים, ג, ג).[4]

ד. **וכי יגור אתך גר** (ויקרא י״ט, ל״ג).
כוללין בתפלה גרי הצדק עם הצדיקים. שנאמר, **והדרת פני זקן**, וסמוך לה **וכי יגור
אתך גר** (מגילה י״ז, ב).[5]

ה. **וכי יגור אתך גר בארצכם.**
אין לי (שמקבלים גרים) אלא בארץ. מניין (שמקבלים גרים גם) בחוץ לארץ? ת״ל **וכי
יגור אתך גר, אתך**, בכל מקום שאתך (יבמות מ״ז, א).[6]

ו. **לא תונו אותו** (שם).
באונאת דברים הכתוב מדבר. כיצד? לא יאמר לו, פה שאכל נבילות וטריפות בא
ללמוד תורה מפני הגבורה! ואם הוא בן גרים לא יאמר לו זכור מעשה אבותיך (בבא
מציעא נ״ח, ב).[7]

ז. המאנה את הגר עובר בשלושה לאוין: **וגר לא תונה** (שמות כ״ב, כ). **וכי יגור אתך גר
לא תונו אותו** (ויקרא י״ט, ל״ג). **ולא תונו איש את עמיתו** (ויקרא כ״ה, י״ז) וגר בכלל
עמיתו הוא (בבא מציעא נ״ט, ב).[8]

ח. **אשר הוצאתי** (ויקרא י״ט, ל״ו).
על תנאי שתקבלו עליכם מצות ציצית. שכל המודה במצות ציצית כאילו מודה
ביציאת מצרים. וכל הכופר במצות ציצית כאילו כופר ביציאת מצרים (ספרי זוטא,
פרשת שלח, פסוק מ״א).[9]

ט. אמר ר׳ אלעזר: לא הגלה הקב״ה את ישראל בין האומות אלא כדי שיתוספו עליהם
גרים (פסחים פ״ז, ב).[10]

י. אמר ר׳ חלבו: קשים גרים לישראל כספחת (יבמות מ״ז, ב; ק״ט, ב).[11]

י״א. **כאזרח** (ויקרא י״ט, ל״ד).
תניא: גר שקיבל עליו כל התורה חוץ מדבר אחד . . . אין מקבלים אותו. מאי טעמא?
דכתיב: **כאזרח**. מה אזרח שקיבל עליו את הכל, אף גר שקיבל עליו את הכל (תורת
כהנים ח, ג).[12]

י״ב. **לא תעשו עול במשפט . . . והין צדק יהיה לכם** (ויקרא י״ט, ל״ה-ל״ו).
מה ת״ל **והין צדק** והלא הין בכלל איפת צדק היה! אלא לומר לך שיהא הן שלך צדק
ולאו שלך צדק (בבא מציעא מ״ט, א).[13]

63

CHAPTER SEVEN:
THE OLD AND THE STRANGER
by Ann Helfgott

(1) מפני שיבה

It has been said that the measure of a humane society is not the way the young are treated, but how the elderly and the infirm are treated. The young are appealing and society has a vested interest in them, in that they represent society's future. The elderly, however, are frightening; they remind us of our own mortality. Furthermore, the infirmities which sometimes come with old age can make a formerly self-sufficient person depend upon others to provide life's necessities. Losing the strength we have is a dismal prospect. In short, the elderly often make us feel uncomfortable.

(2) זקן . . . שיבה

The Torah says מפני שיבה תקום and follows it immediately with והדרת פני זקן. We know that parallelism is characteristic of Biblical expression. The Rabbis knew this too, but they also determined that the Torah, being the word of God, contains nothing superfluous; therefore, any parallelism afforded them the opportunity to learn something new, or something more specific, in regard to the commandment.

The verse under discussion commands us to show respect for the elderly. Now, several questions arise regarding this general commandment. For one thing, are we commanded to show respect for an elderly sinner? Just how do we define שיבה and זקן? Is there a difference between them? Why do we have תקום in one place and והדרת in another? How does one show respect? These are just a few of the questions we may ask here. Students could suggest other questions inspired by the text.

In this excerpt, our Sages disagree on the question, "Should we show respect for the elderly sinner?" The first opinion says that the word זקן qualifies שיבה—and then goes on to define the word זקן. Have the students

64

read *Bemidbar* 11:16-17. Here God takes away some of the spirit which He conferred upon Moses and He confers it upon the זקנים. This is an exegetical גזרה שווה, the second of Rabbi Ishmael's שלש עשרה מידות שהתורה נדרשת בהן. Students should also read *Mishlay* 8:22. Who is speaking here? Wisdom personified! The inference is that wisdom is the oldest of God's creations. Rabbi Yosi brings this verse as a proof text for his interpretation that אין זקן אלא מי שקנה חכמה.

Now what about a זקן who abuses his rank, deliberately walking through crowds so that everyone has to stand up to show deference? That this should not be done is derived from another rule, סמוכין, the juxtaposition of clauses or verses. In this case, the final part of והדרת פני זקן, i.e. זקן, is joined to the first part of the next clause ויראת מאלהיך, giving us the sense that even a זקן (no matter how he is defined) must fear God, Who knows all our thoughts.

Our first opinion used the word זקן to qualify or limit the meaning of the word שיבה, thus excluding the elderly sinner. Issi ben Yehuda disagrees: We must arise before every elderly person. According to him, זקן is different from שיבה, and both a זקן and a שיבה deserve our respect. Why did our Sages decide that the הלכה is according to Issi ben Yehuda?

The teacher may want to have students participate in an informal debate on the issue: Should we arise before all elderly people or just before Sages and saints? In connection with this question we must also ask, what do we do if an elderly stranger comes into the room? Why, in fact, respect old age at all? Does our society respect age? What about advertising? Ask students to bring in magazine advertisements which subtly or not-so-subtly use images of youth or age to sell their products. These days, we are advised to "think young," to "be hip," etc. In fact, it would be a good idea to ask what things or types of people our society does respect. How does this affect our mental and spiritual health?

Deferring to anyone is uncommon these days. Is this good or bad? Can there be too much emphasis on respecting our elders? How much is too much? Why? And in another vein, granted that all muggings are deplorable, is there a difference between mugging a person between the ages of twenty and sixty years, and mugging a person over sixty? Does the vulnerability of the elderly have anything to do with the command to show them respect? What other characteristics of the elderly may inspire this commandment? One of the reasons we respect our teachers is that we value education. What values are we affirming when we respect our elders? Perhaps we are affirming the value of life itself.

Class projects could include visiting a nursing home. This would be especially worthwhile if done on a regular basis. Other ideas: invite someone from your local department of social services to speak to the class on the special needs of, and services offered to, the elderly; have students type interviews of their grandparents or other elderly people and compile these oral histories (you may have a class discussion first to compile a list of suggested questions); invite a retired person to speak to the class on his life style forty years ago and his life style today; hold an informal debate on the topic: Should there be a mandatory retirement age? perhaps for some professions?

It is interesting to note that Rashi, in his commentary on *Vayikra*, 19:32 defines הדור: one should not sit in the elderly person's chair, nor should one contradict him (or her). Students may want to discuss other ways that people show respect.

---

(3)   תלמיד חכם רשע

Here we find a strongly worded statement. It reads, in full: כל תלמיד חכם שאין עומד מפני רבו נקרא רשע ואינו מאריך ימים ותלמודו משתכח. Why did the Rabbis feel so strongly about showing respect for one's teacher? Remember, the Rabbis themselves were both students and teachers. They were developing the oral law to suit changing times, translating generalizations into specifics, elucidating that which is vague, and, in short, transforming Judaism into a way of life which could survive the centuries. In other words, the Rabbis were honoring the transmitters of the teachings which contributed to the survival of our people. Teachers are very important to the Jewish people! Does the respect due to teachers carry with it any additional responsibilities for those teachers? A discussion on this topic could tie it in very nicely with (ג) below. Simply, try to lead students to the conclusion that teachers teach not only by their words, but also by their actions.

It is interesting that nowhere is it stated כל רוצח נקרא רשע. The obvious reason is that it was unnecessary to do so; everyone knew that a רוצח is a רשע; however, a statement similar to ours can be found כל המתפלל אחרי בית הכנסת נקרא רשע (*Berakhot* 6b). Such an action implies scorning the synagogue and the worshippers inside. We see that the Rabbis had standards which were by no means self-evident. What values were they teaching us?

---

(4) מוחלין לו על כל עוונותיו

Here again we see סמוכין. We learn from the juxtaposition of גר to זקן that just as the convert begins life as a Jew with a clean slate, so the Sage who is appointed as a judge begins with a clean slate. Although the rule of juxtaposition seems formalistic, there is a basic similarity between a convert and a judge: both have taken upon themselves a stricter code of conduct. The גר is forgiven past sins because he is considered "reborn" when he becomes a Jew. Of what sins may he have been guilty as a non-Jew? Possibly even עבודה זרה, idolatry! Remind students that Jews are obligated to obey many more מצוות than non-Jews. The Sage who is appointed as a judge also assumes greater responsibilities upon his appointment. As a leader of Israel, all of his affairs must be beyond reproach. The best example of this is Moses' punishment for the incident at the waters of Meribah (*Bemidbar* 20: 1-13). A parallel in our time is the attention given to the financial affairs of public officials. Almost every year we hear of scandals involving elected or appointed public officials. Often, but not always, their crimes involve misuse of their power as public officials. Sometimes such people get into trouble, in part, because of what they say. This, obviously, would not mean trouble for the ordinary citizen. However, our standards must be higher for those in leadership positions.

If the teacher is fortunate enough not to have such an investigation going on when one teaches this chapter, mention might be made of former Secretary of the Interior James Watt, whose tactless and often bigoted remarks offended so many people that he had to resign. Another example is a congressman who recommended for citizenship an immigrant who lived in his home district (there's nothing wrong with that) and who received a sizeable sum of money for doing so. Now, in the daily life of ordinary people, no one would think twice about being paid for providing a totally legal service. However, this congressman had to resign as a result of this action. These examples show us that public officials must follow more rigorous rules of conduct than ordinary citizens. A corollary follows here: any investigation into the conduct of a public official has rendered that official virtually non-functioning for the duration of the investigation, whether or not he will be found guilty.

Obviously, the character and ethics of a person should be scrupulously examined before he is ever elected or appointed to serve the public. An interesting case is that of a policewoman in the Morals Division of the New York Police Department who had posed in the nude for a "skin" magazine *before* she became a policewoman. When this came to light, she was fired. This would make an interesting class discussion: Should she have been fired for something she did (which was not illegal) before she took the job? According to our Sages, all that went before was forgiven. Should she not have been hired in the first place? What if she deliberately deceived the hiring committee concerning her previous employment? Another problem involves where to draw the line between the private, personal life of a public official and that person's public actions.

The backgrounds of the Sages were probably well known to their colleagues before they were considered for appointment as judges. However, it has always been accepted among the Jews that "there lives no man on earth who is so righteous that he sins not." The judge, who has accepted a post which demands an even higher standard of behavior than that of the ordinary Jew, need not suffer for what he did before his appointment.

---

(5)   גרי הצדק

Read על הצדיקים in the *Siddur* in class. Questions for discussion may include: What kinds of people are included in this prayer for God's compassion? What kinds of people are not included? The teacher should lead students to the appreciation that this prayer is for admirable people, not for people who are pathetic or who have problems. Why do we want God to have compassion on such people? What would happen if these righteous people suffered much tragedy (as they often did)? Perhaps others would say, "It is not worth it to be so righteous. God isn't good to the righteous." Also, we just don't like to see good people suffer; it offends our sense of justice, which is an essential part of our Jewishness. Why are גרי הצדק included here? Why is גר qualified by the word צדק? What kind of גר is not a גר צדק? According to R. Nehemiah (*Yevamot* 24b), "A proselyte who converted in order to marry, or who converted in order to enjoy the royal table or to become a servant of Solomon . . . proselytes who converted from fear of the lions (see II *Melakhim* 17: 22-41), proselytes who converted because of dreams, the proselytes of Mordecai and Esther (see *Esther*, chapter 8, especially verse 17) are not (true) proselytes unless they convert . . . as at the present time (i.e., out of inner conviction and without regard to any material benefit)." To be a גר צדק, then, one must convert to Judaism out of deep inner conviction.   We learn to include גר צדק with the others in this prayer from סמוכין—the juxtaposition of והדרת פני זקן and וכי יגור אתך גר. Just as זקני עמך are included, so, too, גרי הצדק are included in our prayer.

68

Now may be a good time to review the three examples of סמוכין in this chapter. The latter two examples (from ג and ד) contain several similarities:

(a) they involve identical phrases (וכי יגור אתך גר and והדרת פני זקן)

(b) they leave each phrase intact

(c) what we know about one subject we apply to the other.

The first example of סמוכין (in א) uses a different technique: it separates the last word of one phrase and then attaches it to the next phrase. (For more on סמוכין see Mielziner: *Introduction to the Talmud*, New York, 1968, Bloch Publishing Company, pp. 177-179.)

---

(6)   בכל מקום שאתך

In the Torah, the word גר means a resident alien. So, in one verse the Torah speaks of the גר in ארץ ישראל and in the next verse reminds us that we were גרים in Egypt. By the time of the Rabbis, however, the word גר meant proselyte, or convert to Judaism. You might want to speculate with the class on how this word changed meaning. Probably the alien residents of ארץ ישראל began to assimilate. Then, wherever and whenever a non-Jew adopted the customs and religion of Israel, he or she was termed a גר (or גיורת).

It is important to understand the plain meaning of the Biblical text first. In our homeland, where we are the majority, we should not oppress a foreigner, or one in the minority. Does this apply to the Arabs in Israel today? Good question! If the class wants to discuss this, one must remember that the גר in ancient Israel was protected, but he did not enjoy all of the rights of citizenship; for example, he was not permitted to own land.

By the time of the Rabbis, ארץ ישראל was under Roman rule and the Jews were persecuted and oppressed in their own land. The term "alien resident" as applied to non-Jews in א״י was meaningless, because the "aliens" had the power. How could we oppress them? Furthermore, the Jewish community outside of א״י (i.e., in the Persian Empire, also known as Babylonia) enjoyed far greater toleration and prosperity, even though they were גרים in the original sense of the word. גר now meant "proselyte." If we substitute the new meaning of the word here, then we come up with: "When a proselyte settles with you in the land, you shall not oppress him." This leaves us with the obvious question, what if a proselyte settles with you *not* in your land? The answer is also obvious: in neither case do we oppress him or her. The Torah source we use for this is the word אתך, with you—wherever you are.

It would be interesting to compare the גר who has adopted the Jewish people and religion under two different sets of circumstances: first, in a thriving Jewish community, and secondly, in a persecuted Jewish community. Would there be a difference in motives in the two situations? Would the גר need different personality traits and strengths of character? Would the Jews regard the proselytes differently in the different situations? For example, in a situation of persecution, Jews may be tempted to mistrust the proselyte as a "spy" for the oppressor. Jews living in prosperity may also be tempted to mistrust the proselyte thinking, "He wants to be one of us when things are going well for us, but what will happen if our fortune changes? How deep is his faith?" And if the punishment for conversion to Judaism is death to both the convert and his teacher, then do the Jews have the obligation to discourage conversion under those circumstances? In spite of mixed feelings toward proselytes, we learn, "Proselytes are beloved in every place. He considers them as part of Israel".

---

(7) לא תונו אותו

This commentary defines the word תונו (root: ינה) which is generally translated as "oppress, cheat, mistreat." How would you translate לא תונו אותו according to this interpretation of the Rabbis? ("Don't taunt him" or something similar.) This may serve to remind the class that every translation is really an interpretation. This is an important reason for studying our sacred texts in their original languages—usually Hebrew or Aramaic.

Now, the question arises: Why is it forbidden to taunt a convert? After all, no bodily harm will result. The answer is (the same reason that it is forbidden to put a stumbling block before the blind or curse the deaf): we must not exploit other people's vulnerability to hurt them. A blind man cannot see the stumbling block, and so he falls; a deaf person cannot hear the curse, and so he cannot do anything to nullify it; and the proselyte's vulnerability is his feeling of not belonging. He is no longer part of the people he grew up with, and he may still feel somewhat outside the people he has adopted. Consideration of a person's feelings is especially important in the case of the גר who is often emotionally vulnerable. What is the reason given for this מצוה? כי גרים הייתם באָרץ מצרים. We know how it feels to be an outsider! This is but an example of the value the Torah places on the distinctly human ability to empathize. Furthermore, our taunting a גר would be an example of "the pot calling the kettle black," since we ourselves are descendants of גרים in both senses of the word: we were alien residents in Egypt and, in the words of the *Haggadah*, מתחלה עובדי עבודה זרה היו אבותינו.

---

(8) עובר בשלשה לאווין

One who mistreats the גר disobeys no fewer than three laws! Have students read *Shemot* 22:20 and *Vayikra* 25:17 as well as our verse, *Vayikra* 19:33. עמיתו is generally translated as fellow-countryman. According to this, the גר is included in that category. Have students compare and contrast the three verses. How are they similar? How are they different? Don't forget to include the context of each verse in the discussion.

---

(9) ציצת . . . מצרים

Read *Vayikra* 19:35-36. What is the relationship between freedom and honest weights and measures? In a free society, are we free to do anything? Obviously not. The מצוה of honest weights and measures serves to prevent a subtle kind of deception that is often difficult to detect. Abraham Chill in his book *The Mitzvot*, sums it up well: "In view of the fact that God brought the Children of Israel out of Egypt in order to teach the world a lesson in honesty and integrity, it follows that a Jew who uses false weights and measures in dealing with either Jew or Gentile denies the lesson of the Exodus" (p. 251).

The phrase אני ה' אלהיכם אשר הוצאתי אתכם מארץ מצרים occurs numerous times in the Torah. (Look in a concordance to the Bible under יצא—then find הוצאתי.) The מצוות associated with this phrase and their connection to the Exodus is an interesting topic for a special report and lends itself to group effort.

---

(10) כדי שיתוספו אליהם גרים

This statement reveals interesting beliefs about both conversion to Judaism and the גלות. Ask students what the Rabbis' attitudes were on the basis of this text. Lead them to the conclusion that:

(a) Israel's mission as "אור לגויים" involves attracting converts to our religion (among other things); and

(b) גלות serves a positive purpose.

Traditionally, we are used to thinking that Judaism discourages proselytes and that the גלות is a punishment for our sins and a national tragedy.

Have students read *Hoshea* 2:25. Separate this verse into its three clauses. R. Elazar and R. Yohanan both deduced the rabbinic statement לא הגלה הקב"ה את ישראל בין האומות אלא כדי שיתוספו אליהם גרים from the same verse in *Hoshea*. R. Elazar deduced this from the first clause in the verse. He said, "A man sows a *se'ah* (of seeds) in order to get a yield of several *kor* (of grain or produce)." Ask students: In this analogy, what does the *se'ah* of seeds represent (the Jewish people)? What does the *kor* of produce represent (our people enlarged by converts)?

R. Yohanan deduced this (לא הגלה . . .) from the rest of the same verse from *Hoshea*. To his mind, ורחמתי את לא רחמה means that the gentiles will be given the opportunity of coming under the wings of the שכינה through Israel's exile. According to Rashi, R. Yohanan deduces it from the last part of the verse: ואמרתי ללא עמי עמי אתה והוא יאמר אלהי.

How did these two Rabbis feel about proselytes? How did they feel about גלות? Do you think that R. Elazar and R. Yohanan would want all Jews to make *aliyah* now that Israel is a Jewish state? Should Jews actively proselytize? Why or why not? Which prooftext is more appropriate? Which is more profound? Poetic?

---

(11) **קשים גרים**

Here we have a negative view of proselytes. R. Helbo's prooftext is *Yisha'yahu* 14:1. Read it with the class. What is the simple meaning of the verse? What is the prophet's attitude to the גר? What does the word ונספחו mean? How is it related to the word ספחת?

Proselytes have complicated Jewish life in three respects:

(a) Some proselytes relapsed and denounced the Jewish people to the foreign ruler. Josephus (*Apion* 2:123) described Hellenist proselytes who apostasized and returned to their evil ways. Many of the first Christians were proselytes who had relapsed. The Jews also had bitter experiences with proselytes in time of war: proselytes and their children often became renegades, slandering Judaism and denouncing Jewish leaders to the foreign powers.

(b) Many times in history, foreign rulers made laws against "Judaizing," and often whole communities would be punished if Judaizing was even suspected. This was especially true in Catholic countries, but also occurred to some extent in Muslim countries.

(c) Some proselytes were just not fully observant Jews. This could weaken the observance of the Jewish people as a whole. This aspect of the problem will be discussed in the next Rabbinic comment. What is the status today? Are proselytes a plus or a minus?

----

(12)   אף גר שקיבל עליו את הכל

The question before us is: Should we be more lenient regarding the observance of the proselyte than regarding that of the born Jew? Of special concern here is the question whether a proselyte is accepted if he observes all of the *mitzvot* except מילה, for this discouraged many men from becoming Jews. The answer, of course, is that the proselyte must undergo circumcision. We see that equality before the law (a revolutionary concept in its day—and for millennia afterward!) had its drawbacks. This is one of the reasons why many rabbis are hesitant to accept converts: if they fail to perform a prescribed ritual, then they are sinning if they are Jews, but not so if they are not Jews. Why make righteous gentiles into sinners?

This question is just as relevant today as it has ever been. What should a rabbi do if a person comes to him feeling a deep sympathy for the Jewish people, wanting to be part of this people, yet saying that he did not intend to keep kosher? Should the rabbi convert the person or not? What if an interfaith couple plan to marry and the rabbi knows that they will do so whether or not the non-Jew converts? Should the rabbi perform the conversion even though he knows that both Jews and non-Jews work on Shabbat? In other words, because one Jew disobeys the Torah, does that make it all right to "create" another Jew who disobeys? And is there a difference if the non-Jewish partner is the man or the woman? (Keep in mind that the children will be Jewish only if the mother is a Jew.) This would be a good topic for role-playing.

The complicating factor today is that most Jews do not perform all of the

73

מצוות. So, in effect, are we demanding that our proselytes become better Jews than we are? Or should we not demand so much from the proselyte? This problem should be studied both from the viewpoint of the individual's conversion and its impact on that person's life and from the viewpoint of the Jewish people. What will become of us if more and more of our people observe less and less? Have students also read *Vayikra* 24:22.

A summary of Jewish attitudes to proselytes would be constructive. It would also be of great benefit to invite a convert to speak to the class about his or her experiences and thoughts before, during, and after the conversion process. Asking students to jot down any question they may have a day or so before the visit, and discussing them at that time, will help focus the students' attention on specific problems of the convert. Hopefully, the guest will make the students more sensitive to the situation of converts in general.

After the visit, a class debate on whether or not Judaism should accept and/or actively seek converts should encourage not only review of the material, but also more research into the subject.

---

(13) לא תעשו עול במשפט

Our Sages first show us that the word הין is superfluous in this verse, thus freeing it to teach us something new. We have here a play on words: הן also means "yes" in Aramaic. Ask students what they think it means to have a הן צדק and a לאו צדק. Answers may vary from a translation such as "an honest 'yes' and 'no'" to explanations such as "say what you mean" or "think carefully before you answer a question or make a decision." Have students generate as many possibilities as they can. Then tell them of R. Kahana's predicament (details have been invented here to facilitate explanation): R. Kahana was given $120 in advance payment for flax; then, the price was ten dollars per bale. He said that he would deliver twelve bales of flax as soon as he could get them. After he received the money, but before he could deliver the flax, the price went up to $15 per bale. Should he deliver twelve bales of flax as he had originally said he would, and so lose money, or should he deliver only eight bales of flax, as the higher price requires? What would you do? What should the law be? The Sages concluded that, because it was an oral agreement, R. Kahana was not obliged to deliver more than eight bales of flax according to law. However, God "will exact vengeance of him who does not stand by his word (and the spirit of the Sages is displeased with him)!"

Should there be a difference if no money were involved? Students can generate situations applicable to their daily life in which standing by their word would be difficult. Sometimes it is truly impossible to stand by one's word. Do you think that standing by one's word was more important to our Sages than it is to the present generation? Standing by one's word is one of many ways to demonstrate a value that our Rabbis have always admired: integrity.